The Killing of Osama bin Laden

The Killing of Osama bin Laden

Seymour M. Hersh

VERSO

London • New York

First published by Verso 2016
© Seymour M. Hersh 2016

The publisher would like to thank the *London Review of Books*, where the
four chapters of this book were first published: Chapter 1, Vol. 37, No. 10,
May 21, 2015; Chapter 2, Vol. 36, No. 8, April 17, 2014; Chapter 3, Vol. 35,
No. 24, December 19, 2013; Chapter 4, Vol. 38, No. 1, January 7, 2016

1 3 5 7 9 10 8 6 4 2

Verso
UK: 6 Meard Street, London W1F 0EG
US: 20 Jay Street, Suite 1010, Brooklyn, NY 11201
versobooks.com

Verso is the imprint of New Left Books

ISBN-13: 978-1-78478-436-2
ISBN-13: 978-1-78478-437-9 (US EBK)
ISBN-13: 978-1-78478-438-6 (UK EBK)

British Library Cataloguing in Publication Data
A catalogue record for this book is available from the British Library

Library of Congress Cataloging-in-Publication Data

Names: Hersh, Seymour M., author.
Title: The killing of Osama Bin Laden / Seymour M. Hersh.
Description: Brooklyn, NY : Verso Books, 2016. | Includes index.
Identifiers: LCCN 2016002833| ISBN 9781784784362 (hardback : alk. paper) |
  ISBN 9781784784379 (US ebook) | ISBN 9781784784386 (UK ebook)
Subjects: LCSH: United States—Foreign relations—2009- | United
  States—Military policy. | Obama, Barack—Influence. | Bin Laden, Osama,
  1957–2011—Assassination.
Classification: LCC E907 .H48 2016 | DDC 327.73009/05—dc23
LC record available at http://lccn.loc.gov/2016002833

Typeset in Sabon by MJ & N Gavan, Truro, Cornwall, UK
Printed in the US by Maple Press

For Christian and the rest of the gang at the *LRB*,
who know what they are doing

Contents

Introduction

The reportage in this collection has a common theme—false steps by an American president who came to office in 2009 after a brilliant campaign in which he spoke of "hope" and "change we can believe in." Political words are just words, as people everywhere in the world have come to understand, but Barack Obama's rhetoric—the first African-American president of the United States—seemed to strike a chord after eight years of George Bush and Dick Cheney. In his first inaugural address, Obama emphasized the rule of law and the rights of man, declaring, "Those ideals still light the word, and we will not give them up for expedience's sake."

Yet he is a president who told the world a series of lies about the killing of Osama bin Laden in May 2011, some of which recklessly put an ally at risk; who in August 2013, sought congressional approval to bomb Syria, while concealing the fact he had been put on notice that the nerve agent allegedly used by Assad didn't match any of those known to be in Syria's arsenal; who secretly authorized the Central Intelligence

Agency to set up a backchannel flow of arms and ammunition, including anti-aircraft missiles, from chaotic post-Qaddafi Libya via Turkey to Syrian rebels, many of them fanatic Islamists; who ignored repeated US and allied intelligence reports throughout early 2013 depicting the Turkish government, led by President Recep Tayyip Erdoğan, as a vital, and hidden, supporter of al-Nusra and ISIS, two extremist militias then engaged in all-out war against Syria. The White House's refusal to deal with reality led the Pentagon's Joint Chiefs to find a way, through America's military partners, to get intelligence and targeting information to the Syrian military—without Obama's knowledge.

Obama's lapses in judgment and integrity in his foreign policy are all the more confounding because he once promised a very different kind of leadership. He spoke elegantly and passionately on issues ranging from racial prejudice and the need for universal health care to the importance of resolving the festering Middle East crisis and closing America's grotesque prison at Guantánamo. He was not a pacifist, as he said many times in different words, but opposed to the rash use of military might. He spoke of ending "the mindset that causes war." In an era of money-driven politics and venal, cynical politicians, he was seen by some as the brightest and best president America could hope for.

How can one explain a politician who put so much energy in pushing through a health care program and a revolutionary nuclear agreement with Iran while taking the deceitful steps mapped out in this book? How could such a high-minded person endorse, as Obama has, the compilation of hit lists made up of suspected terrorists around the world, including American citizens, to be targeted and killed without judicial process?

It's now evident, fifteen years after the 9/11 attacks, that Obama's foreign policy has maintained many of the core elements of the Global War on Terror initiated by his predecessor—assassinations, drone attacks, heavy reliance on special forces, covert operations and, in the case of Afghanistan, the continued use of American ground forces in combat. And, as in the years of Bush and Cheney, there has been no progress, let alone victory, in the fight against terrorism. ISIS has succeeded al-Qaida as the United States' most feared terrorist enemy, one that now reaches deep into Africa and sends shockwaves into Western Europe and America. Obama still views Russia, a nation sharing the same international terrorist enemies as Washington, as an evil empire that must be confronted rather than as an ally. Since 9/11 I have had access to the some of the thinking inside the White House on the War on Terror. I learned early in the Obama presidency that he was prepared to walk away from first principles. His first public act as president took place on January 22, 2009, two days after his inauguration, when he announced that he was returning the nation to the "moral high ground" by signing an executive order calling for the closing, "as soon as practical," of Guantánamo. As of this writing, that has yet to happen, and more than ninety prisoners continue to fester there, with no due process and no accountability, to America's shame.

Obama had described Afghanistan as "the right war" during his campaign and talked about the need for more troops on the ground there. Many of his supporters were not listening, or chose not to hear. I was told that within three weeks of taking office he informed his senior advisers at a secret National Security Council meeting of his plan to send an additional 17,000 American troops to join the 47,000 already stationed there. This outcome was not the product of an interagency staff decision, but a unilateral action taken by Obama and retired marine general James Jones, the national security adviser at the time. Obama and Jones were said to believe that the focus of American foreign policy needed to be on Pakistan, a nuclear power supporting and harboring the Taliban troops that had become the main opponent in Afghanistan after al-Qaida's retreat. There was much hubris and—as usual in new administrations—not much consideration of what had gone before. Furthermore, I was told by someone in a position to know that Jones had explained at one meeting, in essence, that "Afghanistan is not in our national security interest, but we don't want to betray the good men who went there before. We will not abandon Afghanistan, but we will not let it get worse."

Obama would spend much of his first year discussing what to do about Afghanistan. The debate was not about whether to expand the war there but how many troops to commit to what would become America's longest and least successful war. The president, who would spend the rest of his time in office cracking down on press leaks and internal dissent, stood aside as a group of American generals staged what amounted to a public debate over the number of troops needed to "win" the Afghan war. At one point, a highly classified internal request from Army General Stanley McChrystal, an expert on special operations and commander of US forces in the Afghan war, was leaked to the *Washington Post* within a week of its delivery to the White House, with no significant protest or sanction from Obama. McChrystal had asked permission to deploy as many as 80,000 more troops.

Obama eventually committed a first tranche of 30,000 additional American soldiers. It was a decision marketed as a compromise between a reluctant president and a gung-ho Pentagon. There was at least one senior member of Congress who had reason to suspect that Obama, despite his resentment of the military's public posturing, had wanted these higher troop numbers all along.

By 2009, David Obey, a Democratic lawmaker from Wisconsin, was chairman of the powerful House Appropriations Committee, one of two committees responsible for funding all government programs, including secret military and intelligence activities. Elected to Congress in 1969, at the height of the anti–Vietnam War protests, Obey was an outspoken liberal. He had dared to take on George Bush and Dick Cheney over aspects of their war on terror that—as Obey and others in Congress believed—were not being shared with, and perhaps were not even financed by, Congress, as stipulated by the Constitution. Obey got nowhere with his protests, but his efforts in early 2005—including a little-noted speech on the House floor and the solicitation of a rush of unfulfilled promises from the Bush White House to provide greater communication—were remarkable simply for having taken place. He told me at the time that "disquieting" actions had been taken in secret and "Congress has failed in its oversight abilities."

Obey stunned his colleagues in 2010 by announcing his retirement. He and I had talked on and off during the Bush years—he would listen but say little. Six or so months after he left the Congress he was more forthcoming. He told me of a presidential meeting he and a few other congressional leaders had attended at the White House in March 2009. The issue was Afghanistan, and Obama wanted them to know he was going to make a significant troop commitment to the war there. "He said he was being told by a lot of people that he ought to expand the war and then asked all of us, one by one, what we thought. The only word of caution came from [Vice President] Joe Biden, who raised a question about the cost. When it came to me, I said, 'Mr. President, you could have the best policy in the world but you need to have the tools to carry it out—and the governments of Pakistan and Afghanistan are pretty lousy tools. If you did a surge in Afghanistan you will have to face the fact that it would crowd out large portions of your domestic program—except perhaps health care.' " (A later in-house estimate put the cost of the war, if 40,000 additional troops were committed, at $1 trillion over the next ten years, as much as the president's health care proposal.)

At the end of the meeting, according to Obey, he had a private chat with the president, and asked him whether he had ever spent time listening to the broadcasts of President Lyndon Johnson's telephone conversations, in particular his discussions about expanding America's commitment to the war in South Vietnam. Johnson had taped more than 9,000 of his telephone calls while in office. They created a sensation in Washington upon their public release in 2003—just as President Bush was expanding America's war in Iraq. Obama said he had. "I then asked Obama if he recalled listening to the conversation with Richard Russell when they both talked about how upping the American effort in Vietnam wouldn't help," Obey said. "My point was that Johnson and Russell were making a decision to go ahead when they were telling themselves privately that it would not work."

Senator Russell was a segregationist and arch conservative from Georgia, the chairman of the Armed Services Committee, and a longtime Johnson confidant. The conversation in question took place in May 1964, fourteen months before Johnson would make a major commitment of American troops to the war. It remains one of the most riveting and instructive of the presidential recordings. Both men agreed that any American escalation would lead to a major war with China, with untold consequences. "I'll tell you," Russell told Johnson, "it'll be the most expensive adventure this country ever went into." Johnson answered, "It just makes the chills run up my back … I haven't the nerve to do it, but I don't see any other way out of it."

Obey then asked a third question: "Who's your George Ball?" Ball, a high–ranking member of the State Department in the Kennedy years, was renowned as the only senior official in the government to argue again and again—at great personal cost—against Kennedy's decision to escalate the American presence in South Vietnam. Obama did not answer. "Either the president chose not to answer, or he didn't have one," Obey told me. "But I didn't hear anyone tell the president that he ought to put on the brakes in Afghanistan."

In a review of my interviews about Obama's early decision to raise the ante in Afghanistan, one fact stood out: Obama's faith in the world of special operations and in Stanley McChrystal, the commander of US forces in Afghanistan who worked closely with Dick Cheney from 2003 to 2008 as director of the Joint Special Operations Command. JSOC's forces include elite Navy SEALs and the Army's Delta Force, and they have won fame in countless books and movies since 9/11 for their night-time operations against the Taliban in Afghanistan and the jihadists in Iraq. It was a JSOC SEAL team that killed bin Laden at his redoubt in Pakistan in early 2011. There is no ambivalence about the skills and determination of those special operators who took part in Obama's renewed nighttime war against the Taliban in 2009 and thereafter. But, as I was told at the time, there is another side to the elite units. "You've got really good guys who are strongly motivated, and individual initiative is the game," a former senior military official said. "But JSOC's individualism also breeds a group of childish men who take advantage of their operational freedom to act immaturely. 'We're special and the rules don't apply.' This is why the regular army has always tried to limit the size of the special forces. McChrystal was not paid to be thoughtful. He was paid to let his troops do what they want with all the toys to play with they want."

This former senior official, who has been involved in war planning since 9/11, was pessimistic at the time about Obama's reliance on special operations. "The intersection between the high-mindedness of Obama and the ruthlessness of Dick Cheney is so great that there is a vacuum in the planning. And no one knows what will happen. My own belief is that over time we're going to do the Afghanization of the war"—trying, as in Iraq, to finance and train an Afghan Army capable of standing up to the Taliban—"and the same thing will happen to them as happened to our South Vietnamese Army allies. In the end, the Taliban, disciplined and motivated, will take the country back."

McChrystal was cashiered in June 2010, after he and his aides were quoted in *Rolling Stone* making a series of derogatory remarks about the president and others in the White House. Among other comments, McChrystal said an early face-to-face meeting with the president was inconsequential and trivial—little more than a "10-minute photo op." By then, there was much concern about a major aspect of McChrystal's approach to the war, which was to find and kill the Taliban. I was visited that June by a senior official of the International Committee of the Red Cross whose humanitarian mission is to monitor, in secret, the conditions of civilians and prisoners of war in an effort to insure compliance with the 1949 Geneva Conventions. The ICRC was even granted limited access to the prison at Guatánamo, among other facilities in the War on Terror, with the understanding that its findings were not to be made public. The official who sought me out did not want to discuss the prison system in Afghanistan, about which there have been many public revelations. His issue was the Obama administration's overall conduct of the war. He had come to Washington in the hope of seeing Secretary of State Hillary Clinton and other senior State Department officials, but had been shunted aside. His message was blunt: McChrystal's men were killing the wrong people. "Our inspectors are the only visitors from a secular institution who are tolerated by the Taliban leadership, and you Americans are killing those who support our activity," he said. "You are killing those Taliban who are not jihadists—who don't want to die and don't give a shit about bombing Times Square. They have no grudge against America." The indiscriminate targeting of all who are Taliban, he said, "is reaching a point of no return, and the more radical and extreme elements are picking up momentum."

At one point, he said, there had been a heated internal debate among the Taliban leadership about the use of chemical weapons in an attack on Kabul, the Afghan capital, and the moderates won. The ICRC wouldn't say how it learned of that debate, but the official added, "The guys who prevented that use have been smoked out"—assassinated by JSOC operators—"by the Americans. The moderates are going down."

A longtime consultant to the special operations community depicted the mindless killing in Afghanistan as a "symptom of the weakness in the US policy for combatting terrorism: It's all about tactics and nobody, Republican or Democrat, has advanced a strategic vision. The special ops guys are simply carrying out orders, like a dog eager to get off the leash and run in the woods—and not think about where it is going. We've had an abject failure of military and political leadership."

The American-led coalition unilaterally declared an end to the Afghan war at the close of 2014. And, as widely predicted, the Afghanistan Army, supported at an annual cost of billions by the Obama administration, continues to be riddled with corruption and lacks leadership and motivation. Obama again decided last year to send over more troops, under the guise of advisers, and, inevitably, they have been drawn into combat. They kill and are killed in the name of democracy—a word that has dwindling appeal and little relevance for many Afghans.

Did any of the dozens of analyses and estimates put forward as the president reviewed the options in 2009 and in 2015 estimate the number of innocent lives that would be lost as a consequence of the American surge? Were those presidential advisers skeptical of the capability and motivation of an upgraded and modernized Afghan army able to find a place at the White House planning table? Is there an American soldier who wants to be the last to die in Afghanistan?

It is not too early to dwell on Obama's legacy, a deepening concern for any president as the end of his tenure approaches. It would be easy to say it will be mixed—on the plus side there was the health care bill and America's recovery from the economic shambles left by the Bush administration. He faced an unbridgeable congressional impasse caused by an increasingly radical Republican opposition. But Obama, whatever his private thoughts, still speaks of American exceptionalism and still believes, or acts as if he does, that the War on Terror, a war against an ideology, can be won with American bombers, drone attacks and special forces. There is no evidence yet for that belief.

Seymour M. Hersh
Washington, DC
January 15, 2016

The Killing of Osama bin Laden

It's been four years since a group of US Navy SEALS assassinated Osama bin Laden in a night raid on a high-walled compound in Abbottabad, Pakistan. The killing was the high point of Obama's first term, and a major factor in his re-election. The White House still maintains that the mission was an all-American affair, and that the senior generals of Pakistan's army and Inter-Services Intelligence agency (ISI) were not told of the raid in advance. This is false, as are many other elements of the Obama administration's account. The White House's story might have been written by Lewis Carroll: would bin Laden, target of a massive international manhunt, really decide that a resort town forty miles from Islamabad would be the safest place to live and command al-Qaida's operations? He was hiding in the open. So America said.

The most blatant lie was that Pakistan's two most senior military leaders—General Ashfaq Parvez Kayani, chief of the army staff, and General Ahmed Shuja Pasha, director general of the ISI—were never informed of the US mission. This remains the White House position despite an array of reports that have raised questions, including one by Carlotta Gall in the *New York Times Magazine* of March 19, 2014. Gall, who spent 12 years as the *Times* correspondent in Afghanistan, wrote that she'd been told by a "Pakistani official" that Pasha had known before the raid that bin Laden was in Abbottabad. The story was denied by US and Pakistani officials, and went no further. In his book *Pakistan: Before and after Osama* (2012), Imtiaz Gul, executive director of the Centre for Research and Security Studies, a think tank in Islamabad, wrote that he'd spoken to four undercover intelligence officers who—reflecting a widely held local view—asserted that the Pakistani military must have had knowledge of the operation. The issue was raised again in February, when a retired general, Asad Durrani, who was head of the ISI in the early 1990s, told an Al Jazeera interviewer that it was "quite possible" that the senior officers of the ISI did not know where bin Laden had been hiding, "but it was more probable that they did [know]. And the idea was that, at the right time, his location would be revealed. And the right time would have been when you can get the necessary quid pro quo—if you have someone like Osama bin Laden, you are not going to simply hand him over to the United States."

This spring I contacted Durrani and told him in detail what I had learned about the bin Laden assault from American sources: that bin Laden had been a prisoner of the ISI at the Abbottabad compound since 2006; that Kayani and Pasha knew of the raid in advance and had made sure that the two helicopters delivering the SEALS to Abbottabad could cross Pakistani airspace without triggering any alarms; that the CIA did not learn of bin Laden's whereabouts by tracking his couriers, as the White House has claimed since May 2011, but from a former senior Pakistani intelligence officer who betrayed the secret in return for much of the $25 million reward offered by the US, and that, while Obama did order the raid and the SEAL team did carry it out, many other aspects of the administration's account were false.

"When your version comes out—if you do it—people in Pakistan will be tremendously grateful," Durrani told me. "For a long time people have stopped trusting what comes out about bin Laden from the official mouths. There will be some negative political comment and some anger, but people like to be told the truth, and what you've told me is essentially what I have heard from former colleagues who have been on a fact-finding mission since this episode." As a former ISI head, he said, he had been told shortly after the raid by "people in the 'strategic community' who would know" that there had been an informant who had alerted the US to bin Laden's presence in Abbottabad, and that after his killing the US's betrayed promises left Kayani and Pasha exposed.

The major US source for the account that follows is a retired senior intelligence official who was knowledgeable about the initial intelligence about bin Laden's presence in Abbottabad. He also was privy to many aspects of the SEALS' training for the raid and to the various after-action reports. Two other US sources, who had access to corroborating information, have been longtime consultants to the Special Operations Command. I also received information from inside Pakistan about widespread dismay among the senior ISI and military leadership—echoed later by Durrani—over Obama's decision to go public immediately with news of bin Laden's death. The White House did not respond to requests for comment.

It began with a walk-in. In August 2010 a former senior Pakistani intelligence officer approached Jonathan Bank, then the CIA's station chief at the US embassy in Islamabad. He offered to tell the CIA where to find bin Laden in return for the reward that Washington had offered in 2001. Walk-ins are assumed by the CIA to be unreliable, and the response from the agency's headquarters was to fly in a polygraph team. The walk-in passed the test. "So now we've got a lead on bin Laden living in a compound in Abbottabad, but how do we really know who it is?" was the CIA's worry at the time, the retired senior US intelligence official told me.

The US initially kept what it knew from the Pakistanis. "The fear was that if the existence of the source was made known, the Pakistanis themselves would move bin Laden to another location. So only a very small number of people were read into the source and his story," the retired official said. "The CIA's first goal was to check out the quality of the informant's information."

The compound was put under satellite surveillance. The CIA rented a house in Abbottabad to use as a forward observation base and staffed it with Pakistani employees and foreign nationals. Later on, the base would serve as a contact point with the ISI; it attracted little attention because Abbottabad is a holiday spot full of houses rented on short leases. A psychological profile of the informant was prepared. (The informant and his family were smuggled out of Pakistan and relocated in the Washington area. He is now a consultant for the CIA.)

"By October the military and intelligence community were discussing the possible military options. Do we drop a bunker buster on the compound or take him out with a drone strike? Perhaps send someone to kill him, single assassin style? But then we'd have no proof of who he was," the retired official said. "We could see some guy is walking around at night, but we have no intercepts because there's no commo coming from the compound."

In October, Obama was briefed on the intelligence. His response was cautious, the retired official said. "It just made no sense that bin Laden was living in Abbottabad. It was just too crazy. The president's position was emphatic: 'Don't talk to me about this any more unless you have proof that it really is bin Laden.'" The immediate goal of the CIA leadership and the Joint Special Operations Command was to get Obama's support. They believed they would get this if they got DNA evidence and if they could assure him that a night assault of the compound would carry no risk. The only way to accomplish both things, the retired official said, "was to get the Pakistanis on board."

During the late autumn of 2010, the US continued to keep quiet about the walk-in, and Kayani and Pasha continued to insist to their American counterparts that they had no information about bin Laden's whereabouts. "The next step was to figure out how to ease Kayani and Pasha into it—to tell them that we've got intelligence showing that there is a high-value target in the compound, and to ask them what they know about the target," the retired official said. "The compound was not an armed enclave—no machine guns around, because it was under ISI control." The walk-in had told the US that bin Laden had lived undetected from 2001 to 2006 with some of his wives and children in the Hindu Kush mountains, and that "the ISI got to him by paying some of the local tribal people to betray him." (Reports after the raid placed him elsewhere in Pakistan during this period.) Bank was also told by the walk-in that bin Laden was very ill, and that early on in his confinement at Abbottabad, the ISI had ordered Amir Aziz, a doctor and a major in the Pakistani army, to move nearby to provide treatment. "The truth is that bin Laden was an invalid, but we cannot say that," the retired official said. "'You mean you guys shot a cripple? Who was about to grab his AK-47?'"

"It didn't take long to get the cooperation we needed, because the Pakistanis wanted to ensure the continued release of American military aid, a good percentage of which was anti-terrorism funding that finances personal security, such as bullet-proof limousines and security guards and housing for the ISI leadership," the retired official said. He added that there were also under-the-table personal "incentives" that were financed by off-the-books Pentagon contingency funds. "The intelligence community knew what the Pakistanis needed to agree—there was the carrot. And they chose the carrot. It was a win-win. We also did a little blackmail. We told them we would leak the fact that you've got bin Laden in your backyard. We knew their friends and enemies"—the Taliban and jihadist groups in Pakistan and Afghanistan —"would not like it."

A worrying factor at this early point, according to the retired official, was Saudi Arabia, which had been financing bin Laden's upkeep since his seizure by the Pakistanis. "The Saudis didn't want bin Laden's presence revealed to us because he was a Saudi, and so they told the Pakistanis to keep him out of the picture. The Saudis feared if we knew we would pressure the Pakistanis to let bin Laden start talking to us about what the Saudis had been doing with al-Qaida. And they were dropping money—lots of it. The Pakistanis, in turn, were concerned that the Saudis might spill the beans about their control of bin Laden. The fear was that if the US found out about bin Laden from Riyadh, all hell would break out. The Americans learning about bin Laden's imprisonment from a walk-in was not the worst thing."

Despite their constant public feuding, American and Pakistani military and intelligence services have worked together closely for decades on counterterrorism in South Asia. Both services often find it useful to engage in public feuds "to cover their asses," as the retired official put it, but they continually share intelligence used for drone attacks and cooperate on covert operations. At the same time, it's understood in Washington that elements of the ISI believe that maintaining a relationship with the Taliban leadership inside Afghanistan is essential to national security. The ISI's strategic aim is to balance Indian influence in Kabul; the Taliban is also seen in Pakistan as a source of jihadist shock troops who would back Pakistan against India in a confrontation over Kashmir.

Adding to the tension was the Pakistani nuclear arsenal, often depicted in the Western press as an "Islamic bomb" that might be transferred by Pakistan to an embattled nation in the Middle East in the event of a crisis with Israel. The US looked the other way when Pakistan began building its weapons system in the 1970s, and it's widely believed it now has more than a hundred nuclear warheads. It's understood in Washington that US security depends on the maintenance of strong military and intelligence ties to Pakistan. The belief is mirrored in Pakistan.

"The Pakistani army sees itself as family," the retired official said. "Officers call soldiers their sons and all officers are 'brothers.' The attitude is different in the

American military. The senior Pakistani officers believe they are the elite and have got to look out for all of the people, as keepers of the flame against Muslim fundamentalism. The Pakistanis also know that their trump card against aggression from India is a strong relationship with the United States. They will never cut their person-to-person ties with us."

Like all CIA station chiefs, Bank was working undercover, but that ended in early December 2010 when he was publicly accused of murder in a criminal complaint filed in Islamabad by Karim Khan, a Pakistani journalist whose son and brother, according to local news reports, had been killed by a US drone strike. Allowing Bank to be named was a violation of diplomatic protocol on the part of the Pakistani authorities, and it brought a wave of unwanted publicity. Bank was ordered to leave Pakistan by the CIA, whose officials subsequently told the Associated Press he was transferred because of concerns for his safety. The *New York Times* reported that there was "strong suspicion" the ISI had played a role in leaking Bank's name to Khan. There was speculation that he was outed as payback for the publication in a New York lawsuit a month earlier of the names of ISI chiefs in connection with the Mumbai terrorist attacks of 2008. But there was a collateral reason, the retired official said, for the CIA's willingness to send Bank back to America. The Pakistanis needed cover in case their cooperation with the Americans in getting rid of bin Laden became known. The Pakistanis could say: 'You're talking about me? We just kicked out your station chief.' "

The bin Laden compound was less than two miles from the Pakistan Military Academy, and a Pakistani army combat battalion headquarters was another mile or so away. Abbottabad is less than 15 minutes by helicopter from Tarbela Ghazi, an important base for ISI covert operations and the facility where those who guard Pakistan's nuclear weapons arsenal are trained. "Ghazi is why the ISI put bin Laden in Abbottabad in the first place," the retired official said, "to keep him under constant supervision."

The risks for Obama were high at this early stage, especially because there was a troubling precedent: the failed 1980 attempt to rescue the American hostages in Tehran. That failure was a factor in Jimmy Carter's loss to Ronald Reagan. Obama's worries were realistic, the retired official said. "Was bin Laden ever there? Was the whole story a product of Pakistani deception? What about political blowback in case of failure?" After all, as the retired official said, "If the mission fails, Obama's just a black Jimmy Carter and it's all over for re-election."

Obama was anxious for reassurance that the US was going to get the right man. The proof was to come in the form of bin Laden's DNA. The planners turned for help to Kayani and Pasha, who asked Aziz to obtain the specimens. Soon after the raid the press found out that Aziz had been living in a house near the bin Laden compound: local reporters discovered his name in Urdu on a plate on the door. Pakistani officials denied that Aziz had any connection to bin Laden, but the retired official told me that Aziz had been rewarded with a share of the $25 million reward the US had put up because the DNA sample had showed conclusively that it was bin Laden in Abbottabad. (In his subsequent testimony to a Pakistani commission investigating the bin Laden raid, Aziz said that he had witnessed the attack on Abbottabad, but had no knowledge of who was living in the compound and had been ordered by a superior officer to stay away from the scene.)

Bargaining continued over the way the mission would be executed. "Kayani eventually tells us yes, but he says you can't have a big strike force. You have to come in lean and mean. And you have to kill him, or there is no deal," the retired official said. The agreement was struck by the end of January 2011, and Joint Special Operations Command prepared a list of questions to be answered by the Pakistanis: "How can we be assured of no outside intervention? What are the defences inside the compound and its exact dimensions? Where are bin Laden's rooms and exactly how big are they? How many steps in the stairway? Where are the doors to his rooms, and are they reinforced with steel? How thick?" The Pakistanis agreed to permit a four-man American cell—a Navy SEAL, a CIA case officer and two communications specialists—to set up a liaison office at Tarbela Ghazi for the coming assault. By then, the military had constructed a mock-up of the compound in Abbottabad at a secret former nuclear test site in Nevada, and an elite SEAL team had begun rehearsing for the attack.

The US had begun to cut back on aid to Pakistan—to "turn off the spigot," in the retired official's words. The provision of 18 new F-16 fighter aircraft was delayed, and under-the-table cash payments to the senior leaders were suspended. In April 2011 Pasha met the CIA director, Leon Panetta, at agency headquarters. "Pasha got a commitment that the United States would turn the money back on, and we got a guarantee that there would be no Pakistani opposition during the mission," the retired official said. "Pasha also insisted that Washington stop complaining about Pakistan's lack of cooperation with the American war on terrorism." At one point that spring, Pasha offered the Americans a blunt explanation of the reason Pakistan kept bin Laden's capture a secret, and why it was imperative for the ISI role to remain secret: "We needed a hostage to keep tabs on al-Qaida and the Taliban," Pasha said, according to the retired official. "The ISI was using bin Laden as leverage against Taliban and al-Qaida activities inside Afghanistan and Pakistan. They let the Taliban and al-Qaida leadership know that if they ran operations that clashed with the interests of the ISI, they would turn bin Laden over to us. So if it became known that the Pakistanis had worked with us to get bin Laden at Abbottabad, there would be hell to pay."

At one of his meetings with Panetta, according to the retired official and a source within the CIA, Pasha was asked by a senior CIA official whether he saw himself as acting in essence as an agent for al-Qaida and the Taliban. "He answered no, but said the ISI needed to have some control." The message, as the CIA saw it, according to the retired official, was that Kayani and Pasha viewed bin Laden "as a resource, and they were more interested in their [own] survival than they were in the United States."

A Pakistani with close ties to the senior leadership of the ISI told me that "there was a deal with your top guys. We were very reluctant, but it had to be done—not because of personal enrichment, but because all of the American aid programs would be cut off. Your guys said we will starve you out if you don't do it, and the okay was given while Pasha was in Washington. The deal was not only to keep the taps open, but Pasha was told there would be more goodies for us." The Pakistani said that Pasha's visit also resulted in a commitment from the US to give Pakistan "a freer hand" in Afghanistan as it began its military draw-down there. "And so our top dogs justified the deal by saying this is for our country."

Pasha and Kayani were responsible for ensuring that Pakistan's army and air defence command would not track or engage with the US helicopters used on the mission. The American cell at Tarbela Ghazi was charged with coordinating communications between the ISI, the senior US officers at their command post in Afghanistan, and the two Black Hawk helicopters; the goal was to ensure that no stray Pakistani fighter plane on border patrol spotted the intruders and took action to stop them. The initial plan said that news of the raid shouldn't be announced straightaway. All units in the Joint Special Operations Command operate under stringent secrecy and the JSOC leadership believed, as did Kayani and Pasha, that the killing of bin Laden would not be made public for as long as seven days, maybe longer. Then a carefully constructed cover story would be issued: Obama would announce that DNA analysis confirmed that bin Laden had been killed in a drone raid in the Hindu Kush, on Afghanistan's side of the border. The Americans who planned the mission assured Kayani and Pasha that their cooperation would never be made public. It was understood by all that if the Pakistani role became known, there would be violent protests—bin Laden was considered a hero by many Pakistanis—and Pasha and Kayani and their families would be in danger, and the Pakistani army publicly disgraced.

It was clear to all by this point, the retired official said, that bin Laden would not survive: "Pasha told us at a meeting in April that he could not risk leaving bin Laden in the compound now that we know he's there. Too many people in the Pakistani chain of command know about the mission. He and Kayani had to tell the whole story to the directors of the air defense command and to a few local commanders.

"Of course the guys knew the target was bin Laden and he was there under Pakistani control," the retired official said. "Otherwise, they would not have done the mission without air cover. It was clearly and absolutely a premeditated murder." A former SEAL commander, who has led and participated in dozens of similar missions over the past decade, assured me that "we were not going to keep bin Laden alive—to allow the terrorist to live. By law, we know what we're doing inside Pakistan is a homicide. We've come to grips with that. Each one of us, when we do these missions, say to ourselves, 'Let's face it. We're going to commit a murder.' " The White House's initial account claimed that bin Laden had been brandishing a weapon; the story was aimed at deflecting those who questioned the legality of the US administration's targeted assassination program. The US has consistently maintained, despite widely reported remarks by people involved with the mission, that bin Laden would have been taken alive if he had immediately surrendered.

At the Abbottabad compound ISI guards were posted around the clock to keep watch over bin Laden and his wives and children. They were under orders to leave as soon as they heard the rotors of the US helicopters. The town was dark: the electricity supply had been cut off on the orders of the ISI hours before the raid began. One of the Black Hawks crashed inside the walls of the compound, injuring many on board. "The guys knew the TOT [time on target] had to be tight because they would wake up the whole town going in," the retired official said. The cockpit of the crashed Black Hawk, with its communication and navigational gear, had to be destroyed by concussion grenades, and this would create a series of explosions and a fire visible for miles. Two Chinook helicopters had flown from Afghanistan to a nearby Pakistani intelligence base to provide logistical support, and one of them was immediately dispatched to Abbottabad. But because the helicopter had been equipped with a bladder loaded with extra fuel for the two Black Hawks, it first had to be reconfigured as a troop carrier. The crash of the Black Hawk and the need to fly in a replacement were nerve-wracking and time-consuming setbacks, but the SEALs continued with their mission. There was no firefight as they moved into the compound; the ISI guards had gone. "Everyone in Pakistan has a gun and high-profile, wealthy folks like those who live in Abbottabad have armed bodyguards, and yet there were no weapons in the compound," the retired official pointed out. Had there been any opposition, the team would have been highly vulnerable. Instead, the retired official said, an ISI liaison officer flying with the SEALs guided them into the darkened house and up a staircase to bin Laden's quarters. The SEALs had been warned by the Pakistanis that heavy steel doors blocked the stairwell on the first and second-floor landings; bin Laden's rooms were on the third floor. The SEAL squad used explosives to blow the doors open, without injuring anyone. One of bin Laden's wives was screaming hysterically and a bullet—perhaps a stray round—struck her knee. Aside from those that hit bin Laden, no other shots were fired. (The Obama administration's account would hold otherwise.)

"They knew where the target was—third floor, second door on the right," the retired official said. "Go straight there. Osama was cowering and retreated into the bedroom. Two shooters followed him and opened up. Very simple, very straightforward, very professional hit." Some of the SEALs were appalled later at the White House's initial insistence that they had shot bin Laden in self-defense, the retired official said. "Six of the SEALs" finest, most experienced NCOs, faced with an unarmed elderly civilian, had to kill him in self-defense? The house was shabby and bin Laden was living in a cell with bars on the window and barbed wire on the roof. The rules of engagement were that if bin Laden put up any opposition they were authorized to take lethal action. But if they suspected he might have some means of opposition, like an explosive vest under his robe, they could also kill him. So here's this guy in a mystery robe and they shot him. It's not because he was reaching for a weapon. The rules gave them absolute authority to kill the guy." The later White House claim that only one or two bullets were fired into his head was "bullshit," the retired official said. "The squad came through the door and obliterated him. As the SEALs say, 'We kicked his ass and took his gas.' "

After they killed bin Laden, "the SEALs were just there, some with physical injuries from the crash, waiting for the relief chopper," the retired official said. "Twenty tense minutes. The Black Hawk is still burning. There are no city lights. No electricity. No police. No fire trucks. They have no prisoners." Bin Laden's wives and children were left for the ISI to interrogate and relocate. "Despite all the talk," the retired official continued, there were "no garbage bags full of computers and storage devices. The guys just stuffed some books and papers they found in his room in their backpacks. The SEALs weren't there because they thought bin Laden was running a command center for al-Qaida operations, as the White House would later tell the media. And they were not intelligence experts gathering information inside that house."

On a normal assault mission, the retired official said, there would be no waiting around if a chopper went down. "The SEALs would have finished the mission, thrown off their guns and gear, and jammed into the remaining Black Hawk and di-di-maued"—Vietnamese slang for leaving in a rush—"out of there, with guys hanging out of the doors. They would not have blown the chopper—no commo gear is worth a dozen lives—unless they knew they were safe. Instead they stood around outside the compound, waiting for the bus to arrive." Pasha and Kayani had delivered on all their promises.

The backroom argument inside the White House began as soon as it was clear that the mission had succeeded. Bin Laden's body was presumed to be on its way to Afghanistan. Should Obama stand by the agreement with Kayani and Pasha and pretend a week or so later that bin Laden had been killed in a drone attack in the mountains, or should he go public immediately? The downed helicopter made it easy for Obama's political advisers to urge the latter plan. The explosion and fireball would be impossible to hide, and word of what had happened was bound to leak. Obama had to "get out in front of the story" before someone in the Pentagon did: waiting would diminish the political impact.

Not everyone agreed. Robert Gates, the secretary of defense, was the most outspoken of those who insisted that the agreements with Pakistan had to be honored. In his memoir, *Duty*, Gates did not mask his anger:

> Before we broke up and the president headed upstairs to tell the American people what had just happened, I reminded everyone that the techniques, tactics and procedures the SEALs had used in the bin Laden operation were used every night in Afghanistan ... it was therefore essential that we agree not to release any operational details of the raid. That we killed him, I said, is all we needed to say. Everybody in that room agreed to keep mum on details. That commitment lasted about five hours. The initial leaks came from the White House and CIA. They just couldn't wait to brag and to claim credit. The facts were often wrong ... Nonetheless the information just kept pouring out. I was outraged and at one point, told [the national security adviser, Tom] Donilon, "Why doesn't everybody just shut the fuck up?" To no avail.

Obama's speech was put together in a rush, the retired official said, and was viewed by his advisers as a political document, not a message that needed to be submitted for clearance to the national security bureaucracy. This series of self-serving and inaccurate statements would create chaos in the weeks following. Obama said that his administration had discovered that bin Laden was in Pakistan through "a possible lead" the previous August; to many in the CIA the statement suggested a specific event, such as a walk-in. The remark led to a new cover story claiming that the CIA's brilliant analysts had unmasked a courier network handling bin Laden's continuing flow of operational orders to al-Qaida. Obama also praised "a small team of Americans" for their care in avoiding civilian deaths and said: "After a firefight, they killed Osama bin Laden and took custody of his body." Two more details now had to be supplied for the cover story: a description of the firefight that never happened, and a story about what happened to the corpse. Obama went on to praise the Pakistanis: "It's important to note that our counterterrorism cooperation with Pakistan helped lead us to bin Laden and the compound where he was hiding." That statement risked exposing Kayani and Pasha. The White House's solution was to ignore what Obama had said and order anyone talking to the press to insist that the Pakistanis had played no role in killing bin Laden. Obama left the clear impression that he and his advisers hadn't known for sure that bin Laden was in Abbottabad, but only had information "about the possibility." This led first to the story that the SEALs had determined they'd killed the right man by having a six-foot-tall SEAL lie next to the corpse for comparison (bin Laden was known to be six foot four); and then to the claim that a DNA test had been per- formed on the corpse and demonstrated conclusively that the SEALs had killed bin Laden. But, according to the retired official, it wasn't clear from the SEALs' early reports whether all of bin Laden's body, or any of it, made it back to Afghanistan.

Gates wasn't the only official who was distressed by Obama's decision to speak without clearing his remarks in advance, the retired official said, "but he was the only one protesting. Obama didn't just double-cross Gates, he double-crossed everyone. This was not the fog of war. The fact that there was an agreement with the Pakistanis and no contingency analysis of what was to be disclosed if something went wrong—that wasn't even discussed. And once it went wrong, they had to make up a new cover story on the fly." There was a legitimate reason for some deception: the role of the Pakistani walk-in had to be protected.

The White House press corps was told in a brief- ing shortly after Obama's announcement that the death of bin Laden was "the culmination of years of careful and highly advanced intelligence work" that focused on tracking a group of couriers, including one who was known to be close to bin Laden. Reporters were told that a team of specially assembled CIA and National Security Agency analysts had traced the courier to a highly secure million-dollar compound in Abbottabad. After months of observation, the American intelligence community had "high confidence" that a high-value target was living in the compound, and it was "assessed that there was a strong probability that [it] was Osama bin Laden." The US assault team ran into a firefight on entering the compound and three adult males—two of them believed to be the couriers—were slain, along with bin Laden. Asked if bin Laden had defended himself, one of the briefers said yes: "He did resist the assault force. And he was killed in a firefight."

The next day John Brennan, then Obama's senior adviser for counterterrorism, had the task of talking up Obama's valor while trying to smooth over the misstatements in his speech. He provided a more detailed but equally misleading account of the raid and its planning. Speaking on the record, which he rarely does, Brennan said that the mission was carried out by a group of Navy SEALs who had been instructed to take bin Laden alive, if possible. He said the US had no information suggesting that anyone in the Pakistani government or military knew bin Laden's whereabouts: "We didn't contact the Pakistanis until after all of our people, all of our aircraft were out of Pakistani airspace." He emphasized the courage of Obama's decision to order the strike, and said that the White House had no information "that confirmed that bin Laden was at the compound" before the raid began. Obama, he said, "made what I believe was one of the gutsiest calls of any president in recent memory." Brennan increased the number killed by the

SEALs inside the compound to five: bin Laden, a courier, his brother, a bin Laden son, and one of the women said to be shielding bin Laden.

Asked whether bin Laden had fired on the SEALs, as some reporters had been told, Brennan repeated what would become a White House mantra: "He was engaged in a firefight with those that entered the area of the house he was in. And whether or not he got off any rounds, I quite frankly don't know ... Here is bin Laden, who has been calling for these attacks ... living in an area that is far removed from the front, hiding behind women who were put in front of him as a shield ... [It] just speaks to I think the nature of the individual he was."

Gates objected to the idea, pushed by Brennan and Leon Panetta, that US intelligence had learned of bin Laden's whereabouts from information acquired by waterboarding and other forms of torture. "All of this is going on as the SEALs are flying home from their mission. The agency guys know the whole story," the retired official said. "It was a group of annuitants who did it." (Annuitants are retired CIA officers who remain active on contract.) "They had been called in by some of the mission planners in the agency to help with the cover story. So the old-timers come in and say why not admit that we got some of the information about bin Laden from enhanced interrogation?" At the time, there was still talk in Washington about the possible prosecution of CIA agents who had conducted torture.

"Gates told them this was not going to work," the

retired official said. "He was never on the team. He knew at the eleventh hour of his career not to be a party to this nonsense. But State, the agency and the Pentagon had bought in on the cover story. None of the SEALs thought that Obama was going to get on national TV and announce the raid. The Special Forces command was apoplectic. They prided themselves on keeping operational security." There was fear in Special Operations, the retired official said, that "if the true story of the missions leaked out, the White House bureaucracy was going to blame it on the SEALs."

The White House's solution was to silence the SEALs. On May 5, every member of the SEAL hit team—they had returned to their base in southern Virginia—and some members of the Joint Special Operations Command leadership were presented with a nondisclosure form drafted by the White House's legal office; it promised civil penalties and a lawsuit for anyone who discussed the mission, in public or private. "The SEALs were not happy," the retired official said. But most of them kept quiet, as did Admiral William McRaven, who was then in charge of JSOC. "McRaven was apoplectic. He knew he was fucked by the White House, but he's a dyed-in-the-wool SEAL, and not then a political operator, and he knew there's no glory in blowing the whistle on the president. When Obama went public with bin Laden's death, everyone had to scramble around for a new story that made sense, and the planners were stuck holding the bag."

Within days, some of the early exaggerations and distortions had become obvious and the Pentagon issued a series of clarifying statements. No, bin Laden was not armed when he was shot and killed. And no, bin Laden did not use one of his wives as a shield. The press by and large accepted the explanation that the errors were the inevitable by-product of the White House's desire to accommodate reporters frantic for details of the mission.

One lie that has endured is that the SEALs had to fight their way to their target. Only two SEALs have made any public statement: *No Easy Day*, a first-hand account of the raid by Matt Bissonnette, was published in September 2012; and two years later Rob O'Neill was interviewed by Fox News. Both men had resigned from the navy; both had fired at bin Laden. Their accounts contradicted each other on many details, but their stories generally supported the White House version, especially when it came to the need to kill or be killed as the SEALs fought their way to bin Laden. O'Neill even told Fox News that he and his fellow SEALs thought, "We were going to die." "The more we trained on it, the more we realized … this is going to be a one-way mission."

But the retired official told me that in their initial debriefings the SEALs made no mention of a firefight, or indeed of any opposition. The drama and danger portrayed by Bissonnette and O'Neill met a deep-seated need, the retired official said: "SEALs cannot live with the fact that they killed bin Laden totally unopposed, and so there has to be an account of their courage in the face of danger. The guys are going to sit around the bar and say it was an easy day? That's not going to happen."

There was another reason to claim there had been a firefight inside the compound, the retired official said: to avoid the inevitable question that would arise from an uncontested assault. Where were bin Laden's guards? Surely, the most sought-after terrorist in the world would have around-the-clock protection. "And one of those killed had to be the courier, because he didn't exist and we couldn't produce him. The Pakistanis had no choice but to play along with it." (Two days after the raid, Reuters published photographs of three dead men that it said it had purchased from an ISI official. Two of the men were later identified by an ISI spokesman as being the alleged courier and his brother.)

Five days after the raid the Pentagon press corps was provided with a series of videotapes that were said by US officials to have been taken from a large collection the SEALs had removed from the compound, along with as many as 15 computers. Snippets from one of the videos showed a solitary bin Laden looking wan and wrapped in a blanket, watching what appeared to be a video of himself on television. An unnamed official told reporters that the raid produced a "treasure trove ... the single largest collection of senior terrorist materials ever," which would provide vital insights into al-Qaida's plans. The official said the material showed that bin Laden "remained an active leader in al-Qaida, providing strategic, operational and tactical instructions to the group ... He was far from a figurehead [and] continued to direct even tactical details of the group's management and to encourage plotting" from what was described as a command-and-control center in Abbottabad. "He was an active player, making the recent operation even more essential for our nation's security," the official said. The information was so vital, he added, that the administration was setting up an interagency task force to process it: "He was not simply someone who was penning al-Qaida strategy. He was throwing operational ideas out there and he was also specifically directing other al-Qaida members."

These claims were fabrications: there wasn't much activity for bin Laden to exercise command and control over. The retired intelligence official said that the CIA's internal reporting shows that since bin Laden moved to Abbottabad in 2006 only a handful of terrorist attacks could be linked to the remnants of bin Laden's al-Qaida. "We were told at first," the retired official said, "that the SEALs produced garbage bags of stuff and that the community is generating daily intelligence reports out of this stuff. And then we were told that the community is gathering everything together and needs to translate it. But nothing has come of it. Every single thing they have created turns out not to be true. It's a great hoax—like the Piltdown man." The retired official said that most of the materials from Abbottabad were turned over to the US by the Pakistanis, who later razed the building. The

ISI took responsibility for the wives and children of bin Laden, none of whom was made available to the US for questioning.

"Why create the treasure trove story?" the retired official said. "The White House had to give the impression that bin Laden was still operationally important. Otherwise, why kill him? A cover story was created—that there was a network of couriers coming and going with memory sticks and instructions. All to show that bin Laden remained important."

In July 2011, the *Washington Post* published what purported to be a summary of some of these materials. The story's contradictions were glaring. It said the documents had resulted in more than four hundred intelligence reports within six weeks; it warned of unspecified al-Qaida plots; and it mentioned arrests of suspects "who are named or described in emails that bin Laden received." The *Post* didn't identify the suspects or reconcile that detail with the administration's previous assertions that the Abbottabad compound had no Internet connection. Despite their claims that the documents had produced hundreds of reports, the *Post* also quoted officials saying that their main value wasn't the actionable intelligence they contained, but that they enabled "analysts to construct a more comprehensive portrait of al-Qaida."

In May 2012, the Combating Terrorism Center at West Point, a private research group, released translations it had made under a federal government contract of 175 pages of bin Laden documents. Reporters found none of the drama that had been touted in the days after the raid. Patrick Cockburn wrote about the contrast between the administration's initial claims that bin Laden was the "spider at the center of a conspiratorial web" and what the translations actually showed: that bin Laden was "delusional" and had "limited contact with the outside world outside his compound."

The retired official disputed the authenticity of the West Point materials: "There is no linkage between these documents and the counterterrorism center at the agency. No intelligence community analysis. When was the last time the CIA: 1) announced it had a significant intelligence find; 2) revealed the source; 3) described the method for processing the materials; 4) revealed the timeline for production; 5) described by whom and where the analysis was taking place, and 6) published the sensitive results before the information had been acted on? No agency professional would support this fairy tale."

In June 2011, it was reported in the *New York Times*, the *Washington Post* and all over the Pakistani press that Amir Aziz had been held for questioning in Pakistan; he was, it was said, a CIA informant who had been spying on the comings and goings at the bin Laden compound. Aziz was released, but the retired official said that US intelligence was unable to learn who leaked the highly classified information about his involvement with the mission. Officials in Washington decided they "could not take a chance that Aziz's role in obtaining bin Laden's DNA also would become known." A sacrificial lamb was needed, and the one chosen was Shakil Afridi, a forty-eight-year-old Pakistani doctor and sometime CIA asset, who had been arrested by the Pakistanis in late May and accused of assisting the agency. "We went to the Pakistanis and said go after Afridi," the retired official said. "We had to cover the whole issue of how we got the DNA." It was soon reported that the CIA had organized a fake vaccination program in Abbottabad with Afridi's help in a failed attempt to obtain bin Laden's DNA. Afridi's legitimate medical operation was run independently of local health authorities, was well financed and offered free vaccinations against hepatitis B. Posters advertising the program were displayed throughout the area. Afridi was later accused of treason and sentenced to 33 years in prison because of his ties to an extremist. News of the CIA-sponsored program created widespread anger in Pakistan, and led to the cancellation of other international vaccination programs that were now seen as cover for American spying.

The retired official said that Afridi had been recruited long before the bin Laden mission as part of a separate intelligence effort to get information about suspected terrorists in Abbottabad and the surrounding area. "The plan was to use vaccinations as a way to get the blood of terrorism suspects in the villages." Afridi made no attempt to obtain DNA from the residents of the bin Laden compound. The report that he did so was a hurriedly put together "CIA cover story creating 'facts'" in a clumsy attempt to protect Aziz and his real mission. "Now we have the consequences," the retired official said. "A great humanitarian project to do something meaningful for the peasants has been compromised as a cynical hoax." Afridi's conviction was overturned, but he remains in prison on a murder charge.

In his address announcing the raid, Obama said that after killing bin Laden the SEALs "took custody of his body." The statement created a problem. In the initial plan it was to be announced a week or so after the fact that bin Laden was killed in a drone strike somewhere in the mountains on the Pakistan/Afghanistan border and that his remains had been identified by DNA testing. But with Obama's announcement of his killing by the SEALs everyone now expected a body to be produced. Instead, reporters were told that bin Laden's body had been flown by the SEALs to an American military airfield in Jalalabad, Afghanistan, and then straight to the USS *Carl Vinson*, a supercarrier on routine patrol in the North Arabian Sea. Bin Laden had then been buried at sea, just hours after his death. The press corps's only skeptical moments at John Brennan's briefing on May 2 were to do with the burial. The questions were short, to the point, and rarely answered. "When was the decision made that he would be buried at sea if killed?" "Was this part of the plan all along?" "Can you just tell us why that was a good idea?" "John, did you consult a Muslim expert on that?" "Is there a visual recording of this burial?" When this last question was asked, Jay Carney, Obama's press secretary, came to Brennan's rescue: "We've got to give other people a chance here."

"We thought the best way to ensure that his body was given an appropriate Islamic burial," Brennan said, "was to take those actions that would allow us to do that burial at sea." He said "appropriate specialists and experts" were consulted, and that the US military was fully capable of carrying out the burial "consistent with Islamic law." Brennan didn't mention that Muslim law calls for the burial service to be conducted in the presence of an imam, and there was no suggestion that one happened to be on board the *Carl Vinson*.

In a reconstruction of the bin Laden operation for *Vanity Fair*, Mark Bowden, who spoke to many senior administration officials, wrote that bin Laden's body was cleaned and photographed at Jalalabad. Further procedures necessary for a Muslim burial were performed on the carrier, he wrote, "with bin Laden's body being washed again and wrapped in a white shroud. A navy photographer recorded the burial in full sunlight, Monday morning, May 2." Bowden described the photos:

> One frame shows the body wrapped in a weighted shroud. The next shows it lying diagonally on a chute, feet overboard. In the next frame the body is hitting the water. In the next it is visible just below the surface, ripples spreading outward. In the last frame there are only circular ripples on

the surface. The mortal remains of Osama bin Laden were gone for good.

Bowden was careful not to claim that he had actually seen the photographs he described, and he recently told me he hadn't seen them: "I'm always disappointed when I can't look at something myself, but I spoke with someone I trusted who said he had seen them himself and described them in detail." Bowden's statement adds to the questions about the alleged burial at sea, which has provoked a flood of Freedom of Information Act requests, most of which produced no information. One of them sought access to the photographs. The Pentagon responded that a search of all available records had found no evidence that any photographs had been taken of the burial. Requests on other issues related to the raid were equally unproductive. The reason for the lack of response became clear after the Pentagon held an inquiry into allegations that the Obama administration had provided access to classified materials to the makers of the film *Zero Dark Thirty*. The Pentagon report, which was put online in June 2013, noted that Admiral McRaven had ordered the files on the raid to be deleted from all military computers and moved to the CIA, where they would be shielded from FOIA requests by the agency's "operational exemption."

McRaven's action meant that outsiders could not get access to the *Carl Vinson*'s unclassified logs. Logs are sacrosanct in the navy, and separate ones are kept for air operations, the deck, the engineering department, the medical office, and for command information and control. They show the sequence of events day by day aboard the ship; if there has been a burial at sea aboard the *Carl Vinson*, it would have been recorded.

There wasn't any gossip about a burial among the *Carl Vinson*'s sailors. The carrier concluded its six-month deployment in June 2011. When the ship docked at its home base in Coronado, California, Rear Admiral Samuel Perez, commander of the *Carl Vinson* carrier strike group, told reporters that the crew had been ordered not to talk about the burial. Captain Bruce Lindsey, skipper of the *Carl Vinson*, told reporters he was unable to discuss it. Cameron Short, one of the crew of the *Carl Vinson*, told the *Commercial-News* of Danville, Illinois, that the crew had not been told anything about the burial. "All he knows is what he's seen on the news," the newspaper reported.

The Pentagon did release a series of emails to the Associated Press. In one of them, Rear Admiral Charles Gaouette reported that the service followed "traditional procedures for Islamic burial," and said none of the sailors on board had been permitted to observe the proceedings. But there was no indication of who washed and wrapped the body, or of which Arabic speaker conducted the service.

Within weeks of the raid, I had been told by two longtime consultants to Special Operations Command, who have access to current intelligence, that the funeral aboard the *Carl Vinson* didn't take place. One consultant told me that bin Laden's remains were photographed and identified after being flown back to Afghanistan. The consultant added: "At that point, the CIA took control of the body. The cover story was that it had been flown to the *Carl Vinson*." The second consultant agreed that there had been "no burial at sea." He added that "the killing of bin Laden was political theatre designed to burnish Obama's military credentials ... The SEALs should have expected the political grandstanding. It's irresistible to a politician. Bin Laden became a working asset." Early this year, speaking again to the second consultant, I returned to the burial at sea. The consultant laughed and said: "You mean, he didn't make it to the water?"

The retired official said there had been another complication: some members of the SEAL team had bragged to colleagues and others that they had torn bin Laden's body to pieces with rifle fire. The remains, including his head, which had only a few bullet holes in it, were thrown into a body bag and, during the helicopter flight back to Jalalabad, some body parts were tossed out over the Hindu Kush mountains—or so the SEALs claimed. At the time, the retired official said, the SEALs did not think their mission would be made public by Obama within a few hours: "If the president had gone ahead with the cover story, there would have been no need to have a funeral within hours of the killing. Once the cover story was blown, and the death was made public, the White

House had a serious 'Where's the body?' problem. The world knew US forces had killed bin Laden in Abbottabad. Panic city. What to do? We need a 'functional body' because we have to be able to say we identified bin Laden via a DNA analysis. It would be navy officers who came up with the 'burial at sea' idea. Perfect. No body. Honorable burial following sharia law. Burial is made public in great detail, but Freedom of Information documents confirming the burial are denied for reasons of 'national security.' It's the classic unraveling of a poorly constructed cover story—it solves an immediate problem but, given the slightest inspection, there is no back-up support. There never was a plan, initially, to take the body to sea, and no burial of bin Laden at sea took place." The retired official said that if the SEALs' first accounts are to be believed, there wouldn't have been much left of bin Laden to put into the sea in any case.

It was inevitable that the Obama administration's lies, misstatements and betrayals would create a backlash. "We've had a four-year lapse in cooperation," the retired official said. "It's taken that long for the Pakistanis to trust us again in the military-to-military counterterrorism relationship—while terrorism was rising all over the world ... They felt Obama sold them down the river. They're just now coming back because the threat from ISIS, which is now showing up there, is a lot greater and the bin Laden event is far enough away to enable someone like General Durrani to come out and talk about it." Generals Pasha and Kayani have retired and both are reported to be under investigation for corruption during their time in office.

The Senate Intelligence Committee's long-delayed report on CIA torture, released last December, documented repeated instances of official lying, and suggested that the CIA's knowledge of bin Laden's courier was sketchy at best and predated its use of waterboarding and other forms of torture. The report led to international headlines about brutality and waterboarding, along with gruesome details about rectal feeding tubes, ice baths and threats to rape or murder family members of detainees who were believed to be withholding information. Despite the bad publicity, the report was a victory for the CIA. Its major finding—that the use of torture didn't lead to discovering the truth—had already been the subject of public debate for more than a decade. Another key finding—that the torture conducted was more brutal than Congress had been told—was risible, given the extent of public reporting and published exposés by former interrogators and retired CIA officers. The report depicted tortures that were obviously contrary to international law as violations of rules or "inappropriate activities" or, in some cases, "management failures." Whether the actions described constitute war crimes was not discussed, and the report did not suggest that any of the CIA interrogators or their superiors should be investigated for criminal activity. The agency faced no meaningful consequences as a result of the report.

The retired official told me that the CIA leadership had become experts in derailing serious threats from Congress: "They create something that is horrible but not that bad. Give them something that sounds terrible. 'Oh my God, we were shoving food up a prisoner's ass!' Meanwhile, they're not telling the committee about murders, other war crimes, and secret prisons like we still have in Diego Garcia. The goal also was to stall it as long as possible, which they did."

The main theme of the committee's 499-page executive summary is that the CIA lied systematically about the effectiveness of its torture program in gaining intelligence that would stop future terrorist attacks in the US. The lies included some vital details about the uncovering of an al-Qaida operative called Abu Ahmed al-Kuwaiti, who was said to be the key al-Qaida courier, and the subsequent tracking of him to Abbottabad in early 2011. The agency's alleged intelligence, patience and skill in finding al-Kuwaiti became legend after it was dramatized in *Zero Dark Thirty*.

The Senate report repeatedly raised questions about the quality and reliability of the CIA's intelligence about al-Kuwaiti. In 2005 an internal CIA report on the hunt for bin Laden noted that "detainees provide few actionable leads, and we have to consider the possibility that they are creating fictitious characters to distract us or to absolve themselves of direct knowledge about bin Ladin [*sic*]." A CIA cable a year later stated that "we have had no success in eliciting actionable intelligence on bin Laden's location from any detainees." The report also highlighted several instances of CIA officers, including Panetta, making false statements to Congress and the public about the value of "enhanced interrogation techniques" in the search for bin Laden's couriers.

Obama today is not facing re-election as he was in the spring of 2011. His principled stand on behalf of the proposed nuclear agreement with Iran says much, as does his decision to operate without the support of the conservative Republicans in Congress. High-level lying nevertheless remains the modus operandi of US policy, along with secret prisons, drone attacks, Special Forces night raids, bypassing the chain of command, and cutting out those who might say no.

2

The Red Line and the Rat Line

In 2011 Barack Obama led an allied military intervention in Libya without consulting the US Congress. Last August, after the sarin attack on the Damascus suburb of Ghouta, he was ready to launch an allied air strike, this time to punish the Syrian government for allegedly crossing the "red line" he had set in 2012 on the use of chemical weapons (see Chapter 3). Then with less than two days to go before the planned strike, he announced that he would seek congressional approval for the intervention. The strike was postponed as Congress prepared for hearings, and subsequently canceled when Obama accepted Assad's offer to relinquish his chemical arsenal in a deal brokered by Russia. Why did Obama delay and then relent on Syria when he was not shy about rushing into Libya? The answer lies in a clash between those in the administration who were committed to enforcing the red line and military leaders who thought that going to war was both unjustified and potentially disastrous.

Obama's change of mind had its origins at Porton Down, the defense laboratory in Wiltshire. British intelligence had obtained a sample of the sarin used in the August 21 attack and analysis demonstrated that the gas used didn't match the batches known to exist in the Syrian army's chemical weapons arsenal. The message that the case against Syria wouldn't hold up was quickly relayed to the US joint chiefs of staff. The British report heightened doubts inside the Pentagon; the joint chiefs were already preparing to warn Obama that his plans for a far-reaching bomb and missile attack on Syria's infrastructure could lead to a wider war in the Middle East. As a consequence the American officers delivered a last-minute caution to the president, which, in their view, eventually led to his canceling the attack.

For months there had been acute concern among senior military leaders and the intelligence community about the role in the war of Syria's neighbors, especially Turkey. Prime Minister Recep Erdoğan was known to be supporting the al-Nusra Front, a jihadist faction among the rebel opposition, as well as other Islamist rebel groups. "We knew there were some in the Turkish government," a former senior US intelligence official, who has access to current intelligence, told me, "who believed they could get Assad's nuts in a vice by dabbling with a sarin attack inside Syria—and forcing Obama to make good on his red line threat."

The joint chiefs also knew that the Obama administration's public claims that only the Syrian army had access to sarin were wrong. The American and British intelligence communities had been aware since the spring of 2013 that some rebel units in Syria were developing chemical weapons. On June 20 analysts for the US Defense Intelligence Agency issued a highly classified five-page "talking points" briefing for the DIA's deputy director, David Shedd, which stated that al-Nusra maintained a sarin production cell: its program, the paper said, was "the most advanced sarin plot since al-Qaida's pre-9/11 effort." (According to a Defense Department consultant, US intelligence has long known that al-Qaida experimented with chemical weapons, and has a video of one of its gas experiments with dogs.) The DIA paper went on:

> Previous IC [intelligence community] focus had been almost entirely on Syrian CW [chemical weapons] stockpiles; now we see ANF attempting to make its own CW ... Al-Nusrah Front's relative freedom of operation within Syria leads us to assess the group's CW aspirations will be difficult to disrupt in the future.

The paper drew on classified intelligence from numerous agencies: "Turkey and Saudi-based chemical facilitators," it said, "were attempting to obtain sarin precursors in bulk, tens of kilograms, likely for the anticipated large scale production effort in Syria." (Asked about the DIA paper, a spokesperson for the Director of National Intelligence said: "No such paper was ever requested or produced by intelligence community analysts.")

Last May, more than ten members of the al-Nusra Front were arrested in southern Turkey with what local police told the press were two kilograms of sarin. In a 130-page indictment the group was accused of attempting to purchase fuses, piping for the construction of mortars, and chemical precursors for sarin. Five of those arrested were freed after a brief detention. The others, including the ringleader, Haytham Qassab, for whom the prosecutor requested a prison sentence of 25 years, were released pending trial. In the meantime the Turkish press has been rife with speculation that the Erdoğan administration has been covering up the extent of its involvement with the rebels. In a news conference last summer, Aydin Sezgin, Turkey's ambassador to Moscow, dismissed the arrests and claimed to reporters that the recovered "sarin" was merely "anti-freeze."

The DIA paper took the arrests as evidence that al-Nusra was expanding its access to chemical weapons. It said Qassab had "self-identified" as a member of al-Nusra, and that he was directly connected to Abd al-Ghani, the "ANF emir for military manufacturing." Qassab and his associate Khalid Ousta worked with Halit Unalkaya, an employee of a Turkish firm called Zirve Export, who provided "price quotes for bulk quantities of sarin precursors." Abd al-Ghani's plan was for two associates to "perfect a process for making sarin, then go to Syria to train others to begin large scale production at an unidentified lab in Syria." The DIA paper said that one of his operatives had purchased a precursor on the "Baghdad chemical market," which "has supported at least seven CW efforts since 2004."

A series of chemical weapon attacks in March and April 2013 was investigated over the next few months by a special UN mission to Syria. A person with close knowledge of the UN's activity in Syria told me that there was evidence linking the Syrian opposition to the first gas attack, on March 19 in Khan Al-Assal, a village near Aleppo. In its final report in December, the mission said that at least 19 civilians and one Syrian soldier were among the fatalities, along with scores of injured. It had no mandate to assign responsibility for the attack, but the person with knowledge of the UN's activities said: "Investigators interviewed the people who were there, including the doctors who treated the victims. It was clear that the rebels used the gas. It did not come out in public because no one wanted to know."

In the months before the attacks began, a former senior Defense Department official told me, the DIA was circulating a daily classified report known as SYRUP on all intelligence related to the Syrian conflict, including material on chemical weapons. But in the spring, distribution of the part of the report concerning chemical weapons was severely curtailed on the orders of Denis McDonough, the White House chief of staff. "Something was in there that triggered a shit fit by McDonough," the former Defense Department official said. "One day it was a huge deal, and then, after the March and April sarin attacks"—he snapped his fingers—"it's no longer there." The decision to restrict distribution was made as the joint chiefs ordered intensive contingency planning for a possible ground invasion of Syria whose primary objective would be the elimination of chemical weapons.

The former intelligence official said that many in the US national security establishment had long been troubled by the president's red line: "The joint chiefs asked the White House, "What does red line mean? How does that translate into military orders? Troops on the ground? Massive strike? Limited strike?" They tasked military intelligence to study how we could carry out the threat. They learned nothing more about the president's reasoning."

In the aftermath of the August 21 attack Obama ordered the Pentagon to draw up targets for bombing. Early in the process, the former intelligence official said, "the White House rejected 35 target sets provided by the joint chiefs of staff as being insufficiently 'painful' to the Assad regime." The original targets included only military sites and nothing by way of civilian infrastructure. Under White House pressure, the US attack plan evolved into "a monster strike": two wings of B-52 bombers were shifted to airbases close to Syria, and navy submarines and ships equipped with Tomahawk missiles were deployed. "Every day the target list was getting longer," the former intelligence official told me.

> The Pentagon planners said we can't use only Tomahawks to strike at Syria's missile sites because their warheads are buried too far below ground, so the two B-52 air wings with two-thousand-pound bombs were assigned to the mission.

Then we'll need standby search-and-rescue teams to recover downed pilots and drones for target selection. It became huge.

The new target list was meant to "completely eradicate any military capabilities Assad had," the former intelligence official said. The core targets included electric power grids, oil and gas depots, all known logistic and weapons depots, all known command and control facilities, and all known military and intelligence buildings.

Britain and France were both to play a part. On August 29, the day Parliament voted against Cameron's bid to join the intervention, the *Guardian* reported that he had already ordered six RAF Typhoon fighter jets to be deployed to Cyprus, and had volunteered a submarine capable of launching Tomahawk missiles. The French air force—a crucial player in the 2011 strikes on Libya—was deeply committed, according to an account in *Le Nouvel Observateur*; François Hollande had ordered several Rafale fighter-bombers to join the American assault. Their targets were reported to be in western Syria.

By the last days of August the president had given the Joint Chiefs a fixed deadline for the launch. "H hour was to begin no later than Monday morning [September 2], a massive assault to neutralize Assad," the former intelligence official said. So it was a surprise to many when during a speech in the White House Rose Garden on August 31 Obama said that the attack would be put on hold, and he would turn to Congress and put it to a vote.

At this stage, Obama's premise—that only the Syrian army was capable of deploying sarin—was unraveling. Within a few days of the August 21 attack, the former intelligence official told me, Russian military intelligence operatives had recovered samples of the chemical agent from Ghouta. They analyzed it and passed it on to British military intelligence; this was the material sent to Porton Down. (A spokesperson for Porton Down said: "Many of the samples analyzed in the UK tested positive for the nerve agent sarin." MI6 said that it doesn't comment on intelligence matters.)

The former intelligence official said the Russian who delivered the sample to the UK was "a good source—someone with access, knowledge and a record of being trustworthy." After the first reported uses of chemical weapons in Syria last year, American and allied intelligence agencies "made an effort to find the answer as to what, if anything, was used—and its source," the former intelligence official said. "We use data exchanged as part of the Chemical Weapons Convention. The DIA's baseline consisted of knowing the composition of each batch of Soviet-manufactured chemical weapons. But we didn't know which batches the Assad government currently had in its arsenal. Within days of the Damascus incident we asked a source in the Syrian government to give us a list of the batches the government currently had. This is why we could confirm the difference so quickly."

The process hadn't worked as smoothly in the spring, the former intelligence official said, because the studies done by Western intelligence "were inconclusive as to the type of gas it was. The word 'sarin' didn't come up. There was a great deal of discussion about this, but since no one could conclude what gas it was, you could not say that Assad had crossed the president's red line." By August 21, the former intelligence official went on, "the Syrian opposition clearly had learned from this and announced that 'sarin' from the Syrian army had been used, before any analysis could be made, and the press and White House jumped at it. Since it now was sarin, 'It had to be Assad.'"

The UK defense staff who relayed the Porton Down findings to the joint chiefs were sending the Americans a message, the former intelligence official said: "We're being set up here." (This account made sense of a terse message a senior official in the CIA sent in late August: "It was not the result of the current regime. UK & US know this.") By then the attack was a few days away and American, British and French planes, ships and submarines were at the ready.

The officer ultimately responsible for the planning and execution of the attack was General Martin Dempsey, chairman of the joint chiefs. From the beginning of the crisis, the former intelligence official said, the joint chiefs had been sceptical of the administration's argument that it had the facts to back up its belief in Assad's guilt. They pressed the DIA and other agencies for more substantial evidence. "There was no way they thought Syria would use nerve gas at that stage, because

Assad was winning the war," the former intelligence official said. Dempsey had irritated many in the Obama administration by repeatedly warning Congress over the summer of the danger of American military involvement in Syria. Last April, after an optimistic assessment of rebel progress by the secretary of state, John Kerry, in front of the House Foreign Affairs Committee, Dempsey told the Senate Armed Services Committee that "there's a risk that this conflict has become stalemated."

Dempsey's initial view after August 21 was that a US strike on Syria—under the assumption that the Assad government was responsible for the sarin attack—would be a military blunder, the former intelligence official said. The Porton Down report caused the joint chiefs to go to the president with a more serious worry: that the attack sought by the White House would be an unjustified act of aggression. It was the joint chiefs who led Obama to change course. The official White House explanation for the turnabout—the story the press corps told—was that the president, during a walk in the Rose Garden with Denis McDonough, his chief of staff, suddenly decided to seek approval for the strike from a bitterly divided Congress with which he'd been in conflict for years. The former Defense Department official told me that the White House provided a different explanation to members of the civilian leadership of the Pentagon: the bombing had been called off because there was intelligence "that the Middle East would go up in smoke" if it was carried out.

The president's decision to go to Congress was initially seen by senior aides in the White House, the former intelligence official said, as a replay of George W. Bush's gambit in the autumn of 2002 before the invasion of Iraq: "When it became clear that there were no WMD in Iraq, Congress, which had endorsed the Iraqi war, and the White House both shared the blame and repeatedly cited faulty intelligence. If the current Congress were to vote to endorse the strike, the White House could again have it both ways—wallop Syria with a massive attack and validate the president's red line commitment, while also being able to share the blame with Congress if it came out that the Syrian military wasn't behind the attack." The turnabout came as a surprise even to the Democratic leadership in Congress. In September the *Wall Street Journal* reported that three days before his Rose Garden speech Obama had telephoned Nancy Pelosi, leader of the House Democrats, "to talk through the options." She later told colleagues, according to the *Journal*, that she hadn't asked the president to put the bombing to a congressional vote.

Obama's move for congressional approval quickly became a dead end. "Congress was not going to let this go by," the former intelligence official said. "Congress made it known that, unlike the authorization for the Iraq war, there would be substantive hearings." At this point, there was a sense of desperation in the White House, the former intelligence official said. "And so out comes Plan B. Call off the bombing strike and Assad would agree to unilaterally sign the chemical warfare treaty and agree to the destruction of all chemical weapons under UN supervision." At a press conference in London on September 9, Kerry was still talking about intervention: "The risk of not acting is greater than the risk of acting." But when a reporter asked if there was anything Assad could do to stop the bombing, Kerry said: "Sure. He could turn over every single bit of his chemical weapons to the international community in the next week … But he isn't about to do it, and it can't be done, obviously." As the *New York Times* reported the next day, the Russian-brokered deal that emerged shortly afterwards had first been discussed by Obama and Putin in the summer of 2012. Although the strike plans were shelved, the administration didn't change its public assessment of the justification for going to war. "There is zero tolerance at that level for the existence of error," the former intelligence official said of the senior officials in the White House. "They could not afford to say: 'We were wrong.'" (The Director of National Intelligence spokesperson said: "The Assad regime, and only the Assad regime, could have been responsible for the chemical weapons attack that took place on August 21.")

The full extent of US cooperation with Turkey, Saudi Arabia and Qatar in assisting the rebel opposition in Syria has yet to come to light. The Obama administration has never publicly admitted to its role in creating what the CIA calls a "rat line," a backchannel highway into Syria. The rat line, authorized in early 2012, was used to funnel weapons and ammunition from Libya via southern Turkey and across the Syrian border to the opposition. Many of those in Syria who ultimately received the weapons were jihadists, some of them affiliated with al-Qaida. (The DNI spokesperson said: "The idea that the United States was providing weapons from Libya to anyone is false.")

In January, the Senate Intelligence Committee released a report on the assault by a local militia in September 2012 on the American consulate and a nearby undercover CIA facility in Benghazi, which resulted in the death of the US ambassador, Christopher Stevens, and three others. The report's criticism of the State Department for not providing adequate security at the consulate, and of the intelligence community for not alerting the US military to the presence of a CIA outpost in the area, received front-page coverage and revived animosities in Washington, with Republicans accusing Obama and Hillary Clinton of a cover-up. A highly classified annex to the report, not made public, described a secret agreement reached in early 2012 between the Obama and Erdoğan administrations. It pertained to the rat line. By the terms of the agreement, funding came from Turkey, as well as Saudi Arabia and Qatar; the CIA, with the support of MI6, was responsible for getting arms from Gaddafi's arsenals into Syria. A number of front companies were set up in Libya, some under the cover of Australian entities. Retired American soldiers, who didn't always know who was really employing them, were hired to manage procurement and shipping. The operation was run by David Petraeus, the CIA director who would soon resign when it became known he was having an affair with his biographer. (A spokesperson for Petraeus denied the operation ever took place.)

At the time it was set up, the operation had not been disclosed to the congressional intelligence committees and the congressional leadership, as required by law since the 1970s. The involvement of MI6 enabled the CIA to evade the law by classifying the mission as a liaison operation. The former intelligence official explained that for years there has been a recognized exception in the law that permits the CIA not to report liaison activity to Congress, which would otherwise be owed a finding. (All proposed CIA covert operations must be described in a written document, known as a "finding," submitted to the senior leadership of Congress for approval.) Distribution of the annex was limited to the staff aides who wrote the report and to the eight ranking members of Congress—the Democratic and Republican leaders of the House and Senate, and the Democratic and Republicans leaders on the House and Senate intelligence committees. This hardly constituted a genuine attempt at oversight: the eight leaders are not known to gather together to raise questions or discuss the secret information they receive.

The annex didn't tell the whole story of what happened in Benghazi before the attack, nor did it explain why the American consulate was attacked. "The consulate's only mission was to provide cover for the moving of arms," the former intelligence official, who has read the annex, said. "It had no real political role."

Washington abruptly ended the CIA's role in the transfer of arms from Libya after the attack on the consulate, but the rat line kept going. "The United States was no longer in control of what the Turks were relaying to the jihadists," the former intelligence official said. Within weeks, as many as forty portable surface-to-air missile launchers, commonly known as MANPADS (man-portable air-defense systems), were in the hands of Syrian rebels. On November 28, 2012, Joby Warrick of the *Washington Post* reported that the previous day rebels near Aleppo had used what was almost certainly a MANPADS to shoot down a Syrian transport helicopter. "The Obama administration," Warrick wrote, "has steadfastly opposed arming Syrian opposition forces with such missiles, warning that the weapons could fall into the hands of terrorists and be used to shoot down commercial aircraft." Two Middle Eastern intelligence officials fingered Qatar as the source, and a former US intelligence analyst speculated that the MANPADS could have been obtained from Syrian military outposts overrun by the rebels. There was no indication that the rebels' possession of MANPADS was likely the unintended consequence of a covert US program that was no longer under US control.

By the end of 2012, it was believed throughout the

American intelligence community that the rebels were losing the war. "Erdoğan was pissed," the former intelligence official said, "and felt he was left hanging on the vine. It was his money and the cut-off was seen as a betrayal." In spring 2013 US intelligence learned that the Turkish government—through elements of the MIT, its national intelligence agency, and the Gendarmerie, a militarized law-enforcement organization—was working directly with al-Nusra and its allies to develop a chemical warfare capability. "The MIT was running the political liaison with the rebels, and the Gendarmerie handled military logistics, on-the-scene advice and training—including training in chemical warfare," the former intelligence official said. "Stepping up Turkey's role in spring 2013 was seen as the key to its problems there. Erdoğan knew that if he stopped his support of the jihadists it would be all over. The Saudis could not support the war because of logistics—the distances involved and the difficulty of moving weapons and supplies. Erdoğan's hope was to instigate an event that would force the US to cross the red line. But Obama didn't respond in March and April."

There was no public sign of discord when Erdoğan and Obama met on May 16, 2013, at the White House. At a later press conference Obama said that they had agreed that Assad "needs to go." Asked whether he thought Syria had crossed the red line, Obama acknowledged that there was evidence such weapons had been used, but added, "it is important for us to make sure that we're able to get more specific information about what exactly is happening there." The red line was still intact.

An American foreign policy expert who speaks regularly with officials in Washington and Ankara told me about a working dinner Obama held for Erdoğan during his May visit. The meal was dominated by the Turks' insistence that Syria had crossed the red line and their complaints that Obama was reluctant to do anything about it. Obama was accompanied by John Kerry and Tom Donilon, the national security adviser who would soon leave the job. Erdoğan was joined by Ahmet Davutoğlu, Turkey's foreign minister, and Hakan Fidan, the head of the MIT. Fidan is known to be fiercely loyal to Erdoğan, and has been seen as a consistent backer of the radical rebel opposition in Syria.

The foreign policy expert told me that the account he heard originated with Donilon. (It was later corroborated by a former US official, who learned of it from a senior Turkish diplomat.) According to the expert, Erdoğan had sought the meeting to demonstrate to Obama that the red line had been crossed and had brought Fidan along to state the case. When Erdoğan tried to draw Fidan into the conversation, and Fidan began speaking, Obama cut him off and said: "We know." Erdoğan tried to bring Fidan in a second time, and Obama again cut him off and said: "We know." At that point, an exasperated Erdoğan said, "But your red line has been crossed!" and, the expert told me, "Donilon said Erdoğan 'fucking waved his finger at the president inside the White House.' " Obama then pointed at Fidan and said: "We know what you're doing with the radicals in Syria." (Donilon, who joined the Council on Foreign Relations last July, didn't respond to questions about this story. The Turkish Foreign Ministry didn't respond to questions about the dinner. A spokesperson for the National Security Council confirmed that the dinner took place and provided a photograph showing Obama, Kerry, Donilon, Erdoğan, Fidan and Davutoğlu sitting at a table. "Beyond that," she said, "I'm not going to read out the details of their discussions.")

But Erdoğan did not leave empty-handed. Obama was still permitting Turkey to continue to exploit a loophole in a presidential executive order prohibiting the export of gold to Iran, part of the US sanctions regime against the country. In March 2012, responding to sanctions of Iranian banks by the EU, the SWIFT electronic payment system, which facilitates cross-border payments, expelled dozens of Iranian financial institutions, severely restricting the country's ability to conduct international trade. The US followed with the executive order in July, but left what came to be known as a "golden loophole": gold shipments to private Iranian entities could continue. Turkey is a major purchaser of Iranian oil and gas, and it took advantage of the loophole by depositing its energy payments in Turkish lira in an Iranian account in Turkey; these funds were then used to purchase Turkish gold for export to confederates in Iran. Gold to the value of $13 billion reportedly entered Iran in this way between March 2012 and July 2013.

The program quickly became a cash cow for corrupt politicians and traders in Turkey, Iran and the United Arab Emirates. "The middlemen did what they always do," the former intelligence official said. "Take 15 percent. The CIA had estimated that there was as much as $2 billion in skim. Gold and Turkish lira were sticking to fingers." The illicit skimming flared into a public "gas for gold" scandal in Turkey in December, and resulted in charges against two dozen people, including prominent businessmen and relatives of government officials, as well as the resignations of three ministers, one of whom called for Erdoğan to resign. The chief executive of a Turkish state-controlled bank that was in the middle of the scandal insisted that more than $4.5 million in cash found by police in shoeboxes during a search of his home was for charitable donations.

Late last year Jonathan Schanzer and Mark Dubowitz reported in *Foreign Policy* that the Obama administration closed the golden loophole in January 2013, but "lobbied to make sure the legislation ... did not take effect for six months." They speculated that the administration wanted to use the delay as an incentive to bring Iran to the bargaining table over its nuclear program, or to placate its Turkish ally in the Syrian civil war. The delay permitted Iran to "accrue billions of dollars more in gold, further undermining the sanctions regime."

The American decision to end CIA support of the weapons shipments into Syria left Erdoğan exposed politically and militarily. "One of the issues at that May summit was the fact that Turkey is the only avenue to supply the rebels in Syria," the former intelligence official said. "It can't come through Jordan because the terrain in the south is wide open and the Syrians are all over it. And it can't come through the valleys and hills of Lebanon— you can't be sure who you'd meet on the other side." Without US military support for the rebels, the former intelligence official said, "Erdoğan's dream of having a client state in Syria is evaporating and he thinks we're the reason why. When Syria wins the war, he knows the rebels are just as likely to turn on him—where else can they go? So now he will have thousands of radicals in his backyard."

A US intelligence consultant told me that a few weeks before August 21 he saw a highly classified briefing prepared for Dempsey and the defense secretary, Chuck Hagel, which described "the acute anxiety" of the Erdoğan administration about the rebels' dwindling prospects. The analysis warned that the Turkish leadership had expressed "the need to do something that would precipitate a US military response." By late summer, the Syrian army still had the advantage over the rebels, the former intelligence official said, and only American air power could turn the tide. In the autumn, the former intelligence official went on, the US intelligence analysts who kept working on the events of August 21 "sensed that Syria had not done the gas attack. But the 500-pound gorilla was, how did it happen? The immediate suspect was the Turks, because they had all the pieces to make it happen."

As intercepts and other data related to the August 21 attacks were gathered, the intelligence community saw evidence to support its suspicions. "We now know it was a covert action planned by Erdoğan's people to push Obama over the red line," the former intelligence official said. "They had to escalate to a gas attack in or near Damascus when the UN inspectors"—who arrived in Damascus on August 18 to investigate the earlier use of gas—"were there. The deal was to do something spectacular. Our senior military officers have been told by the DIA and other intelligence assets that the sarin was supplied through Turkey—that it could only have gotten there with Turkish support. The Turks also provided the training in producing the sarin and handling it." Much of the support for that assessment came from the Turks themselves, via intercepted conversations in the immediate aftermath of the attack. "Principal evidence came from the Turkish post-attack joy and back-slapping in numerous intercepts. Operations are always so super-secret in the planning but that all flies out the window when it comes to crowing afterwards. There is no greater vulnerability than in the perpetrators claiming credit for success." Erdoğan's problems in Syria would soon be over: "Off goes the gas and Obama will say red line and America is going to attack Syria, or at least that was the idea. But it did not work out that way."

The post-attack intelligence on Turkey did not make

its way to the White House. "Nobody wants to talk about all this," the former intelligence official told me. "There is great reluctance to contradict the president, although no all-source intelligence community analysis supported his leap to convict. There has not been one single piece of additional evidence of Syrian involvement in the sarin attack produced by the White House since the bombing raid was called off. My government can't say anything because we have acted so irresponsibly. And since we blamed Assad, we can't go back and blame Erdoğan."

Turkey's willingness to manipulate events in Syria to its own purposes seemed to be demonstrated late last month, a few days before a round of local elections, when a recording, allegedly of a government national security meeting, was posted to YouTube. It included discussion of a false-flag operation that would justify an incursion by the Turkish military in Syria. The operation centered on the tomb of Suleyman Shah, the grandfather of the revered Osman I, founder of the Ottoman Empire, which is near Aleppo and was ceded to Turkey in 1921, when Syria was under French rule. One of the Islamist rebel factions was threatening to destroy the tomb as a site of idolatry, and the Erdoğan administration was publicly threatening retaliation if harm came to it. According to a Reuters report of the leaked conversation, a voice alleged to be Fidan's spoke of creating a provocation: "Now look, my commander, if there is to be justification, the justification is I send four men to the other side. I get them to fire eight missiles into empty land [in the vicinity of the tomb]. That's not a problem. Justification can be created." The Turkish government acknowledged that there had been a national security meeting about threats emanating from Syria, but said the recording had been manipulated. The government subsequently blocked public access to YouTube.

Barring a major change in policy by Obama, Turkey's meddling in the Syrian civil war is likely to go on. "I asked my colleagues if there was any way to stop Erdoğan's continued support for the rebels, especially now that it's going so wrong," the former intelligence official told me. "The answer was: 'We're screwed.' We could go public if it was somebody other than Erdoğan, but Turkey is a special case. They're a NATO ally. The Turks don't trust the West. They can't live with us if we take any active role against Turkish interests. If we went public with what we know about Erdoğan's role with the gas, it'd be disastrous. The Turks would say: 'We hate you for telling us what we can and can't do.' "

3

Whose Sarin?

Barack Obama did not tell the whole story this autumn when he tried to make the case that Bashar al-Assad was responsible for the chemical weapons attack near Damascus on August 21. In some instances, he omitted important intelligence, and in others he presented assumptions as facts. Most significant, he failed to acknowledge something known to the US intelligence community: that the Syrian army is not the only party in the country's civil war with access to sarin, the nerve agent that a UN study concluded—without assessing responsibility—had been used in the rocket attack. In the months before the attack, the American intelligence agencies produced a series of highly classified reports, culminating in a formal Operations Order—a planning document that precedes a ground invasion—citing evidence that the al-Nusra Front, a jihadi group affiliated with al-Qaida, had mastered the mechanics of creating sarin and was capable of manufacturing it in quantity. When the attack occurred al-Nusra should have been a suspect, but the administration cherry-picked intelligence to justify a strike against Assad.

In his nationally televised speech about Syria on September 10, Obama laid the blame for the nerve gas attack on the rebel-held suburb of Eastern Ghouta firmly on Assad's government, and made it clear he was prepared to back up his earlier public warnings that any use of chemical weapons would cross a "red line": "Assad's government gassed to death over a thousand people," he said. "We know the Assad regime was responsible ... And that is why, after careful deliberation, I determined that it is in the national security interests of the United States to respond to the Assad regime's use of chemical weapons through a targeted military strike." Obama was going to war to back up a public threat, but he was doing so without knowing for sure who did what in the early morning of August 21.

He cited a list of what appeared to be hard-won evidence of Assad's culpability: "In the days leading up to August 21st, we know that Assad's chemical weapons personnel prepared for an attack near an area where they mix sarin gas. They distributed gas masks to their troops. Then they fired rockets from a regime-controlled area into 11 neighborhoods that the regime has been trying to wipe clear of opposition forces." Obama's certainty was echoed at the time by Denis McDonough, his chief of staff, who told the *New York Times*: "No one with whom I've spoken doubts the intelligence" directly linking Assad and his regime to the sarin attacks.

But in recent interviews with intelligence and military officers and consultants past and present, I found intense concern, and on occasion anger, over what was repeatedly seen as the deliberate manipulation of intelligence. One high-level intelligence officer, in an email to a colleague, called the administration's assurances of Assad's responsibility a "ruse." The attack "was not the result of the current regime," he wrote. A former senior intelligence official told me that the Obama administration had altered the available information—in terms of its timing and sequence—to enable the president and his advisers to make intelligence retrieved days after the attack look as if it had been picked up and analyzed in real time, as the attack was happening. The distortion, he said, reminded him of the 1964 Gulf of Tonkin incident, when the Johnson administration reversed the sequence of National Security Agency intercepts to justify one of the early bombings of North Vietnam. The same official said there was immense frustration inside the military and intelligence bureaucracy: "The guys are throwing their hands in the air and saying, 'How can we help this guy'—Obama—'when he and his cronies in the White House make up the intelligence as they go along?'"

The complaints focus on what Washington did not have: any advance warning from the assumed source of the attack. The military intelligence community has for years produced a highly classified early morning intelligence summary, known as the Morning Report, for the secretary of defense and the chairman of the Joint Chiefs of Staff; a copy also goes to the national security adviser and the director of national intelligence. The

Morning Report includes no political or economic information, but provides a summary of important military events around the world, with all available intelligence about them. A senior intelligence consultant told me that some time after the attack he reviewed the reports for August 20 through August 23. For two days—August 20 and 21—there was no mention of Syria. On August 22 the lead item in the Morning Report dealt with Egypt; a subsequent item discussed an internal change in the command structure of one of the rebel groups in Syria. Nothing was noted about the use of nerve gas in Damascus that day. It was not until August 23 that the use of sarin became a dominant issue, although hundreds of photographs and videos of the massacre had gone viral within hours on YouTube, Facebook and other social media sites. At this point, the administration knew no more than the public.

Obama left Washington early on August 21 for a hectic two-day speaking tour in New York and Pennsylvania; according to the White House press office, he was briefed later that day on the attack, and the growing public and media furore. The lack of any immediate inside intelligence was made clear on August 22, when Jen Psaki, a spokesperson for the State Department, told reporters: "We are unable to conclusively determine [chemical weapons] use. But we are focused every minute of every day since these events happened ... on doing everything possible within our power to nail down the facts." The administration's tone had hardened by

August 27, when Jay Carney, Obama's press secretary, told reporters—without providing any specific information—that any suggestions that the Syrian government was not responsible "are as preposterous as suggestions that the attack itself didn't occur."

The absence of immediate alarm inside the American intelligence community demonstrates that there was no intelligence about Syrian intentions in the days before the attack. And there are at least two ways the US could have known about it in advance: both were touched on in one of the top secret American intelligence documents that have been made public in recent months by Edward Snowden, the former NSA contractor.

On August 29, the *Washington Post* published excerpts from the annual budget for all national intelligence programs, agency by agency, provided by Snowden. In consultation with the Obama administration, the newspaper chose to publish only a slim portion of the 178-page document, which has a classification higher than top secret, but it summarized and published a section dealing with problem areas. One problem area was the gap in coverage targeting Assad's office. The document said that the NSA's worldwide electronic eavesdropping facilities had been "able to monitor unencrypted communications among senior military officials at the outset of the civil war there." But it was "a vulnerability that President Bashar al-Assad's forces apparently later recognized." In other words, the NSA no longer had access to the conversations of the top military leadership in Syria, which would have included crucial communications from Assad, such as orders for a nerve gas attack. (In its public statements since August 21, the Obama administration has never claimed to have specific information connecting Assad himself to the attack.)

The *Post* report also provided the first indication of a secret sensor system inside Syria, designed to provide early warning of any change in status of the regime's chemical weapons arsenal. The sensors are monitored by the National Reconnaissance Office, the agency that controls all US intelligence satellites in orbit. According to the *Post* summary, the NRO is also assigned "to extract data from sensors placed on the ground" inside Syria. The former senior intelligence official, who had direct knowledge of the program, told me that NRO sensors have been implanted near all known chemical warfare sites in Syria. They are designed to provide constant monitoring of the movement of chemical warheads stored by the military. But far more important, in terms of early warning, is the sensors' ability to alert US and Israeli intelligence when warheads are being loaded with sarin. (As a neighboring country, Israel has always been on the alert for changes in the Syrian chemical arsenal, and works closely with American intelligence on early warnings.) A chemical warhead, once loaded with sarin, has a shelf life of a few days or less—the nerve agent begins eroding the rocket almost immediately: it's a use-it-or-lose-it mass killer. "The Syrian army doesn't have three days to prepare for a chemical attack," the former senior intelligence official told me. "We created the sensor system for immediate reaction, like an air raid warning or a fire alarm. You can't have a warning over three days because everyone involved would be dead. It is either right now or you're history. You do not spend three days getting ready to fire nerve gas." The sensors detected no movement in the months and days before August 21, the former official said. It is of course possible that sarin had been supplied to the Syrian army by other means, but the lack of warning meant that Washington was unable to monitor the events in Eastern Ghouta as they unfolded.

The sensors had worked in the past, as the Syrian leadership knew all too well. Last December the sensor system picked up signs of what seemed to be sarin production at a chemical weapons depot. It was not immediately clear whether the Syrian army was simulating sarin production as part of an exercise (all militaries constantly carry out such exercises) or actually preparing an attack. At the time, Obama publicly warned Syria that using sarin was "totally unacceptable"; a similar message was also passed by diplomatic means. The event was later determined to be part of a series of exercises, according to the former senior intelligence official: "If what the sensors saw last December was so important that the president had to call and say, 'Knock it off,' why didn't the president issue the same warning three days before the gas attack in August?"

The NSA would of course monitor Assad's office around the clock if it could, the former official said.

Other communications—from various army units in combat throughout Syria—would be far less important, and not analyzed in real time. "There are literally thousands of tactical radio frequencies used by field units in Syria for mundane routine communications," he said, "and it would take a huge number of NSA cryptological technicians to listen in—and the useful return would be zilch." But the "chatter" is routinely stored on computers. Once the scale of events on August 21 was understood, the NSA mounted a comprehensive effort to search for any links to the attack, sorting through the full archive of stored communications. A keyword or two would be selected and a filter would be employed to find relevant conversations. "What happened here is that the NSA intelligence weenies started with an event—the use of sarin—and reached to find chatter that might relate," the former official said. "This does not lead to a high confidence assessment, unless you start with high confidence that Bashar Assad ordered it, and began looking for anything that supports that belief." The cherry-picking was similar to the process used to justify the Iraq war.

The White House needed nine days to assemble its case against the Syrian government. On August 30 it invited a select group of Washington journalists (at least one often critical reporter, Jonathan Landay, the national security correspondent for McClatchy Newspapers, was not invited), and handed them a document carefully labeled as a "government assessment," rather than as an assessment by the intelligence community. The document laid out what was essentially a political argument to bolster the administration's case against the Assad government. It was, however, more specific than Obama would be later, in his speech on September 10: American intelligence, it stated, knew that Syria had begun "preparing chemical munitions" three days before the attack. In an aggressive speech later that day, John Kerry provided more details. He said that Syria's "chemical weapons personnel were on the ground, in the area, making preparations" by August 18. "We know that the Syrian regime elements were told to prepare for the attack by putting on gas masks and taking precautions associated with chemical weapons." The government assessment and Kerry's comments made it seem as if the administration had been tracking the sarin attack as it happened. It is this version of events, untrue but unchallenged, that was widely reported at the time.

An unforeseen reaction came in the form of complaints from the Free Syrian Army's leadership and others about the lack of warning. "It's unbelievable they did nothing to warn people or try to stop the regime before the crime," Razan Zaitouneh, an opposition member who lived in one of the towns struck by sarin, told *Foreign Policy*. The *Daily Mail* was more blunt: "Intelligence report says US officials knew about nerve-gas attack in Syria three days before it killed over 1,400 people—including more than 400 children." (The number of deaths attributable to the attack varied widely, from at least 1,429, as initially claimed by the Obama administration, to many fewer. A Syrian human rights group reported 502 deaths; Médicins sans Frontières put it at 355; and a French report listed 281 known fatalities. The strikingly precise US total was later reported by the *Wall Street Journal* to have been based not on an actual body count, but on an extrapolation by CIA analysts, who scanned more than a hundred YouTube videos from Eastern Ghouta into a computer system and looked for images of the dead. In other words, it was little more than a guess.)

Five days later, a spokesman for the Office of the Director of National Intelligence responded to the complaints. A statement to the Associated Press said that the intelligence behind the earlier administration assertions was not known at the time of the attack, but recovered only subsequently: "Let's be clear, the United States did not watch, in real time, as this horrible attack took place. The intelligence community was able to gather and analyze information after the fact and determine that elements of the Assad regime had in fact taken steps to prepare prior to using chemical weapons." But since the American press corps had their story, the retraction received scant attention. On August 31 the *Washington Post*, relying on the government assessment, had vividly reported on its front page that American intelligence was able to record "each step" of the Syrian army attack in real time, "from the extensive preparations to the launching of rockets to the after-action assessments by Syrian officials." It did not publish the AP corrective, and the White House maintained control of the narrative.

So when Obama said on September 10 that his administration knew Assad's chemical weapons personnel had prepared the attack in advance, he was basing the statement not on an intercept caught as it happened, but on communications analyzed days after August 21. The former senior intelligence official explained that the hunt for relevant chatter went back to the exercise detected the previous December, in which, as Obama later said to the public, the Syrian army mobilized chemical weapons personnel and distributed gas masks to its troops. The White House's government assessment and Obama's speech were not descriptions of the specific events leading up to the August 21 attack, but an account of the sequence the Syrian military would have followed for any chemical attack. "They put together a back story," the former official said, "and there are lots of different pieces and parts. The template they used was the template that goes back to December." It is possible, of course, that Obama was unaware that this account was obtained from an analysis of Syrian army protocol for conducting a gas attack, rather than from direct evidence. Either way he had come to a hasty judgment.

The press would follow suit. The UN report on September 16 confirming the use of sarin was careful to note that its investigators' access to the attack sites, which came five days after the gassing, had been controlled by rebel forces. "As with other sites," the report warned, "the locations have been well traveled by other individuals prior to the arrival of the mission ... During the time spent at these locations, individuals arrived carrying other suspected munitions indicating that such potential evidence is being moved and possibly manipulated." Still, the *New York Times* seized on the report, as did American and British officials, and claimed that it provided crucial evidence backing up the administration's assertions. An annex to the UN report reproduced YouTube photographs of some recovered munitions, including a rocket that "indicatively matches" the specifics of a 330mm caliber artillery rocket. The *New York Times* wrote that the existence of the rockets essentially proved that the Syrian government was responsible for the attack "because the weapons in question had not been previously documented or reported to be in possession of the insurgency."

Theodore Postol, a professor of technology and national security at MIT, reviewed the UN photos with a group of his colleagues and concluded that the large-caliber rocket was an improvised munition that was very likely manufactured locally. He told me that it was "something you could produce in a modestly capable machine shop." The rocket in the photos, he added, fails to match the specifications of a similar but smaller rocket known to be in the Syrian arsenal. The *New York Times*, again relying on data in the UN report, also analyzed the flight path of two of the spent rockets that were believed to have carried sarin, and concluded that the angle of descent "pointed directly" to their being fired from a Syrian army base more than nine kilometers from the landing zone. Postol, who has served as the scientific adviser to the chief of naval operations in the Pentagon, said that the assertions in the *Times* and elsewhere "were not based on actual observations." He concluded that the flight path analyses in particular were, as he put it in an email, "totally nuts" because a thorough study demonstrated that the range of the improvised rockets was "unlikely" to be more than two kilometers. Postol and a colleague, Richard M. Lloyd, published an analysis two weeks after August 21 in which they correctly assessed that the rockets involved carried a far greater payload of sarin than previously estimated. The *Times* reported on that analysis at length, describing Postol and Lloyd as "leading weapons experts." The pair's later study about the rockets' flight paths and range, which contradicted previous *Times* reporting, was emailed to the newspaper last week; it has so far gone unreported.

The White House's misrepresentation of what it knew about the attack, and when, was matched by its readiness to ignore intelligence that could undermine the narrative. That information concerned al-Nusra, the Islamist rebel group designated by the US and the UN as a terrorist organization. Al-Nusra is known to have carried out scores of suicide bombings against Christians and other non-Sunni Muslim sects inside Syria, and to have attacked its nominal ally in the civil war, the secular Free

Syrian Army (FSA). Its stated goal is to overthrow the Assad regime and establish sharia law. (On September 25 al-Nusra joined several other Islamist rebel groups in repudiating the FSA and another secular faction, the Syrian National Coalition.)

The flurry of American interest in al-Nusra and sarin stemmed from a series of small-scale chemical weapons attacks in March and April; at the time, the Syrian government and the rebels each insisted the other was responsible. The UN eventually concluded that four chemical attacks had been carried out, but did not assign responsibility. A White House official told the press in late April that the intelligence community had assessed "with varying degrees of confidence" that the Syrian government was responsible for the attacks. Assad had crossed Obama's "red line." The April assessment made headlines, but some significant caveats were lost in translation. The unnamed official conducting the briefing acknowledged that intelligence community assessments "are not alone sufficient." "We want," he said, "to investigate above and beyond those intelligence assessments to gather facts so that we can establish a credible and corroborated set of information that can then inform our decision-making." In other words, the White House had no direct evidence of Syrian army or government involvement, a fact that was only occasionally noted in the press coverage. Obama's tough talk played well with the public and Congress, who view Assad as a ruthless murderer.

Two months later, a White House statement announced a change in the assessment of Syrian culpability and declared that the intelligence community now had "high confidence" that the Assad government was responsible for as many as 150 deaths from attacks with sarin. More headlines were generated and the press was told that Obama, in response to the new intelligence, had ordered an increase in nonlethal aid to the Syrian opposition. But once again there were significant caveats. The new intelligence included a report that Syrian officials had planned and executed the attacks. No specifics were provided, nor were those who provided the reports identified. The White House statement said that laboratory analysis had confirmed the use of sarin, but also that a positive finding of the nerve agent "does not tell us how or where the individuals were exposed or who was responsible for the dissemination." The White House further declared: "We have no reliable corroborated reporting to indicate that the opposition in Syria has acquired or used chemical weapons." The statement contradicted evidence that at the time was streaming into US intelligence agencies.

Already by late May, the senior intelligence consultant told me, the CIA had briefed the Obama administration on al-Nusra and its work with sarin, and had sent alarming reports that another Sunni fundamentalist group active in Syria, al-Qaida in Iraq (AQI), also understood the science of producing sarin. At the time, al-Nusra was operating in areas close to Damascus, including Eastern

Ghouta. An intelligence document issued in mid-summer dealt extensively with Ziyaad Tariq Ahmed, a chemical weapons expert formerly of the Iraqi military, who was said to have moved into Syria and to be operating in Eastern Ghouta. The consultant told me that Tariq had been identified "as an al-Nusra guy with a track record of making mustard gas in Iraq and someone who is implicated in making and using sarin." He is regarded as a high-profile target by the American military.

On June 20 a four-page top secret cable summarizing what had been learned about al-Nusra's nerve gas capabilities was forwarded to David R. Shedd, deputy director of the Defense Intelligence Agency. "What Shedd was briefed on was extensive and comprehensive," the consultant said. "It was not a bunch of 'we believes.'" He told me that the cable made no assessment as to whether the rebels or the Syrian army had initiated the attacks in March and April, but it did confirm previous reports that al-Nusra had the ability to acquire and use sarin. A sample of the sarin that had been used was also recovered —with the help of an Israeli agent—but, according to the consultant, no further reporting about the sample showed up in cable traffic.

Independently of these assessments, the Joint Chiefs of Staff, assuming that US troops might be ordered into Syria to seize the government's stockpile of chemical agents, called for an all-source analysis of the potential threat. "The Op Order provides the basis of execution of a military mission, if so ordered," the former senior intelligence official explained. "This includes the possible need to send American soldiers to a Syrian chemical site to defend it against rebel seizure. If the jihadist rebels were going to overrun the site, the assumption is that Assad would not fight us because we were protecting the chemical from the rebels. All Op Orders contain an intelligence threat component. We had technical analysts from the Central Intelligence Agency, the Defense Intelligence Agency, weapons people, and I & W [indications and warnings] people working on the problem ... They concluded that the rebel forces were capable of attacking an American force with sarin because they were able to produce the lethal gas. The examination relied on signals and human intelligence, as well as the expressed intention and technical capability of the rebels."

There is evidence that during the summer some members of the Joint Chiefs of Staff were troubled by the prospect of a ground invasion of Syria as well as by Obama's professed desire to give rebel factions non-lethal support. In July, General Martin Dempsey, chairman of the Joint Chiefs, provided a gloomy assessment, telling the Senate Armed Services Committee in public testimony that "thousands of special operations forces and other ground forces" would be needed to seize Syria's widely dispersed chemical warfare arsenal, along with "hundreds of aircraft, ships, submarines and other enablers." Pentagon estimates put the number of troops at 70,000, in part because US forces would also have to guard the Syrian rocket fleet: accessing large volumes of the chemicals that create sarin without the means to deliver it would be of little value to a rebel force. In a letter to Senator Carl Levin, Dempsey cautioned that a decision to grab the Syrian arsenal could have unintended consequences: "We have learned from the past ten years, however, that it is not enough to simply alter the balance of military power without careful consideration of what is necessary in order to preserve a functioning state ... Should the regime's institutions collapse in the absence of a viable opposition, we could inadvertently empower extremists or unleash the very chemical weapons we seek to control."

The CIA declined to comment for this article. Spokesmen for the DIA and Office of the Director of National Intelligence said they were not aware of the report to Shedd and, when provided with specific cable markings for the document, said they were unable to find it. Shawn Turner, head of public affairs for the ODNI, said that no American intelligence agency, including the DIA, "assesses that the al-Nusra Front has succeeded in developing a capacity to manufacture sarin."

The administration's public affairs officials are not as concerned about al-Nusra's military potential as Shedd has been in his public statements. In late July, he gave an alarming account of al-Nusra's strength at the annual Aspen Security Forum in Colorado. "I count no less than 1,200 disparate groups in the opposition," Shedd said, according to a recording of his presentation. "And within the opposition, the al-Nusra Front is ... most effective and is gaining in strength." This, he said, "is of serious concern to us. If left unchecked, I am very concerned that the most radical elements"—he also cited al-Qaida in Iraq—"will take over." The civil war, he went on, "will only grow worse over time ... Unfathomable violence is yet to come." Shedd made no mention of chemical weapons in his talk, but he was not allowed to: the reports his office received were highly classified.

A series of secret dispatches from Syria over the summer reported that members of the FSA were complaining to American intelligence operatives about repeated attacks on their forces by al-Nusra and al-Qaida fighters. The reports, according to the senior intelligence consultant who read them, provided evidence that the FSA is "more worried about the crazies than it is about Assad." The FSA is largely composed of defectors from the Syrian army. The Obama administration, committed to the end of the Assad regime and continued support for the rebels, has sought in its public statements since the attack to downplay the influence of Salafist and Wahhabist factions. In early September, John Kerry dumbfounded a congressional hearing with a sudden claim that al-Nusra and other Islamist groups were minor players in the Syrian opposition. He later withdrew the claim.

In both its public and private briefings after August 21, the administration disregarded the available intelligence about al-Nusra's potential access to sarin and continued to claim that the Assad government was in sole possession of chemical weapons. This was the message conveyed in the various secret briefings that members of Congress received in the days after the attack, when Obama was seeking support for his planned missile offensive against Syrian military installations. One legislator with more than two decades of experience in military affairs told me that he came away from one such briefing persuaded that "only the Assad government had sarin and the rebels did not." Similarly, following the release of the UN report on September 16 confirming that sarin was used on August 21, Samantha Power, the US ambassador to the UN, told a press conference: "It's very important to note that only the [Assad] regime possesses sarin, and we have no evidence that the opposition possesses sarin."

It is not known whether the highly classified reporting on al-Nusra was made available to Power's office, but her comment was a reflection of the attitude that swept through the administration. "The immediate assumption was that Assad had done it," the former senior intelligence official told me. "The new director of the CIA, [John] Brennan, jumped to that conclusion … drives to the White House and says: 'Look at what I've got!' It was all verbal; they just waved the bloody shirt. There was a lot of political pressure to bring Obama to the table to help the rebels, and there was wishful thinking that this [tying Assad to the sarin attack] would force Obama's hand: 'This is the Zimmermann telegram of the Syrian rebellion and now Obama can react.' Wishful thinking by the Samantha Power wing within the administration. Unfortunately, some members of the Joint Chiefs who were alerted that he was going to attack weren't so sure it was a good thing."

The proposed American missile attack on Syria never won public support, and Obama turned quickly to the UN and the Russian proposal for dismantling the Syrian chemical warfare complex. Any possibility of military action was definitively averted on September 26 when the administration joined Russia in approving a draft UN resolution calling on the Assad government to get rid of its chemical arsenal. Obama's retreat brought relief to many senior military officers. (One high-level special operations adviser told me that the ill-conceived American missile attack on Syrian military airfields and missile emplacements, as initially envisaged by the White House, would have been "like providing close air support for al-Nusra.")

The administration's distortion of the facts surrounding the sarin attack raises an unavoidable question: do we have the whole story of Obama's willingness to walk away from his "red line" threat to bomb Syria? He had claimed to have an iron-clad case but suddenly agreed to take the issue to Congress, and later to accept Assad's offer to relinquish his chemical weapons. It appears possible that at some point he was directly confronted with contradictory information: evidence strong enough to persuade him to cancel his attack plan, and take the criticism sure to come from Republicans.

The UN resolution, which was adopted on September 27 by the Security Council, dealt indirectly with the notion that rebel forces such as al-Nusra would also be obliged to disarm: "no party in Syria should use, develop, produce, acquire, stockpile, retain or transfer [chemical] weapons." The resolution also calls for the immediate notification of the Security Council in the event that any "non-state actors" acquire chemical weapons. No group was cited by name. While the Syrian regime continues the process of eliminating its chemical arsenal, the irony is that, after Assad's stockpile of precursor agents is destroyed, al-Nusra and its Islamist allies could end up as the only faction inside Syria with access to the ingredients that can create sarin, a strategic weapon that would be unlike any other in the war zone. There may be more to negotiate.

4

Military to Military

Barack Obama's repeated insistence that Bashar al-Assad must leave office—and that there are "moderate" rebel groups in Syria capable of defeating him—has in recent years provoked quiet dissent, and even overt opposition, among some of the most senior officers on the Pentagon's Joint Staff. Their criticism has focused on what they see as the administration's fixation on Assad's primary ally, Vladimir Putin. In their view, Obama is captive to Cold War thinking about Russia and China, and hasn't adjusted his stance on Syria to the fact both countries share Washington's anxiety about the spread of terrorism in and beyond Syria; like Washington, they believe that Islamic State must be stopped.

The military's resistance dates back to the summer of 2013, when a highly classified assessment, put together by the Defense Intelligence Agency (DIA) and the Joint Chiefs of Staff, then led by General Martin Dempsey, forecast that the fall of the Assad regime would lead to chaos and, potentially, to Syria's takeover by jihadi extremists, much as was then happening in Libya. A former senior adviser to the Joint Chiefs told me that the document was an "all-source" appraisal, drawing on information from signals, satellite and human intelligence, and took a dim view of the Obama administration's insistence on continuing to finance and arm the so-called moderate rebel groups. By then, the CIA had been conspiring for more than a year with allies in the UK, Saudi Arabia and Qatar to ship guns and goods—to be used for the overthrow of Assad—from Libya, via Turkey, into Syria. The new intelligence estimate singled out Turkey as a major impediment to Obama's Syria policy. The document showed, the adviser said, "that what was started as a covert US program to arm and support the moderate rebels fighting Assad had been coopted by Turkey, and had morphed into an across-the-board technical, arms and logistical program for all of the opposition, including Jabhat al-Nusra and Islamic State. The so-called moderates had evaporated and the Free Syrian Army was a rump group stationed at an airbase in Turkey." The assessment was bleak: there was no viable "moderate" opposition to Assad, and the US was arming extremists.

Lieutenant General Michael Flynn, director of the DIA between 2012 and 2014, confirmed that his agency had sent a constant stream of classified warnings to the civilian leadership about the dire consequences of toppling Assad. The jihadists, he said, were in control of the opposition. Turkey wasn't doing enough to stop the smuggling of foreign fighters and weapons across the border. "If the American public saw the intelligence we were producing daily, at the most sensitive level, they would go ballistic," Flynn told me. "We understood Isis's long-term strategy and its campaign plans, and we also discussed the fact that Turkey was looking the other way when it came to the growth of the Islamic State inside Syria." The DIA's reporting, he said, "got enormous pushback" from the Obama administration. "I felt that they did not want to hear the truth."

"Our policy of arming the opposition to Assad was unsuccessful and actually having a negative impact," the former JCS adviser said. "The Joint Chiefs believed that Assad should not be replaced by fundamentalists. The administration's policy was contradictory. They wanted Assad to go but the opposition was dominated by extremists. So who was going to replace him? To say Assad's got to go is fine, but if you follow that through—therefore anyone is better. It's the 'anybody else is better' issue that the JCS had with Obama's policy." The Joint Chiefs felt that a direct challenge to Obama's policy would have "had a zero chance of success." So in the autumn of 2013 they decided to take steps against the extremists without going through political channels, by providing US intelligence to the militaries of other nations, on the understanding that it would be passed on to the Syrian army and used against the common enemy, Jabhat al-Nusra and Islamic State.

Germany, Israel and Russia were in contact with the Syrian army and able to exercise some influence over Assad's decisions—it was through them that US intelligence would be shared. Each had its reasons for cooperating with Assad: Germany feared what might happen among its own population of 6 million Muslims if Islamic State expanded; Israel was concerned with border security; Russia had an alliance of very long standing with Syria, and was worried by the threat to its only naval base on the Mediterranean, at Tartus. "We weren't intent on deviating from Obama's stated policies," the adviser said. "But sharing our assessments via the military-to-military relationships with other countries could prove productive. It was clear that Assad needed better tactical intelligence and operational advice. The JCS concluded that if those needs were met, the overall fight against Islamist terrorism would be enhanced. Obama didn't know, but Obama doesn't know what the JCS does in every circumstance, and that's true of all presidents."

Once the flow of US intelligence began, Germany, Israel and Russia started passing on information about the whereabouts and intent of radical jihadist groups to the Syrian army; in return, Syria provided information about its own capabilities and intentions. There was no direct contact between the US and the Syrian military; instead, the adviser said, "We provided the information—including long-range analyses on Syria's future put together by contractors or one of our war colleges—and these countries could do with it what they chose, including sharing it with Assad. We were saying to the Germans and the others: 'Here's some information that's pretty interesting and our interest is mutual.' End of conversation. The JCS could conclude that something beneficial would arise from it—but it was a military to military thing, and not some sort of a sinister Joint Chiefs' plot to go around Obama and support Assad. It was a lot cleverer than that. If Assad remains in power, it will not be because we did it. It's because he was smart enough to use the intelligence and sound tactical advice we provided to others."

The public history of relations between the US and Syria over the past few decades has been one of enmity. Assad condemned the 9/11 attacks, but opposed the Iraq War. George W. Bush repeatedly linked Syria to the three members of his "axis of evil"—Iraq, Iran and North Korea—throughout his presidency. State Department cables made public by WikiLeaks show that the Bush administration tried to destabilize Syria and that these efforts continued into the Obama years. In December 2006, William Roebuck, then in charge of the US embassy in Damascus, filed an analysis of the "vulner-abilities" of the Assad government and listed methods "that will improve the likelihood" of opportunities for destabilization. He recommended that Washington work with Saudi Arabia and Egypt to increase sectarian tension and focus on publicizing "Syrian efforts against extremist groups"—dissident Kurds and radical Sunni factions—"in a way that suggests weakness, signs of instability, and uncontrolled blowback"; and that the "isolation of Syria" should be encouraged through US support of the National Salvation Front, led by Abdul Halim Khaddam, a former Syrian vice president whose government-in-exile in Riyadh was sponsored by the Saudis and the Muslim Brotherhood. Another 2006 cable showed that the embassy had spent $5 million financing dissidents who ran as independent candidates for the People's Assembly; the payments were kept up even after it became clear that Syrian intelligence knew what was going on. A 2010 cable warned that funding for a London-based television network run by a Syrian opposition group would be viewed by the Syrian government "as a covert and hostile gesture toward the regime."

But there is also a parallel history of shadowy co-operation between Syria and the US during the same period. The two countries collaborated against al-Qaida, their common enemy. A longtime consultant to America's intelligence community said that, after 9/11, "Bashar was, for years, extremely helpful to us while, in my view, we were churlish in return, and clumsy in our use of the gold he gave us. That quiet cooperation continued among some elements, even after the [Bush administration's] decision to vilify him." In 2002 Assad authorized Syrian intelligence to turn over hundreds of internal files on the activities of the Muslim Brotherhood in Syria and Germany. Later that year, Syrian intelligence foiled an attack by al-Qaida on the headquarters of the US Navy's Fifth Fleet in Bahrain, and Assad agreed to provide the CIA with the name of a vital al-Qaida informant. In violation of this agreement, the CIA contacted the informant directly; he rejected the approach, and broke off relations with his Syrian handlers. Assad also secretly turned over to the US relatives of Saddam Hussein who had sought refuge in Syria, and—like America's allies in Jordan, Egypt, Thailand and elsewhere—tortured suspected terrorists for the CIA in a Damascus prison.

It was this history of cooperation that made it seem possible in 2013 that Damascus would agree to the new indirect intelligence-sharing arrangement with the US. The Joint Chiefs let it be known that in return the US would require four things: Assad must restrain Hizbullah from attacking Israel; he must renew the stalled negotiations with Israel to reach a settlement on the Golan Heights; he must agree to accept Russian and other outside military advisers; and he must commit to holding open elections after the war with a wide range of factions included. "We had positive feedback from the Israelis, who were willing to entertain the idea, but they needed to know what the reaction would be from Iran and Syria," the JCS adviser told me. "The Syrians told us that Assad would not make a decision unilaterally —he needed to have support from his military and Alawite allies. Assad's worry was that Israel would say yes and then not uphold its end of the bargain." A senior adviser to the Kremlin on Middle East affairs told me that in late 2012, after suffering a series of battlefield setbacks and military defections, Assad had approached Israel via a contact in Moscow and offered to reopen the talks on the Golan Heights. The Israelis had rejected the offer. "They said, 'Assad is finished,' " the Russian official told me. " 'He's close to the end.' " He said the Turks had told Moscow the same thing. By mid-2013, however, the Syrians believed the worst was behind them and wanted assurances that the Americans and others were serious about their offers of help.

In the early stages of the talks, the adviser said, the Joint Chiefs tried to establish what Assad needed as a sign of their good intentions. The answer was sent through one of Assad's friends: "Bring him the head of Prince Bandar." The Joint Chiefs did not oblige. Bandar bin Sultan had served Saudi Arabia for decades in intelligence and national security affairs, and spent more than twenty years as ambassador in Washington. In recent years, he has been known as an advocate for Assad's removal from office by any means. Reportedly in poor health, he resigned last year as director of the Saudi National Security Council, but Saudi Arabia continues to be a major provider of funds to the Syrian opposition, estimated by US intelligence last year at $700 million.

In July 2013, the Joint Chiefs found a more direct way of demonstrating to Assad how serious they were about helping him. By then the CIA-sponsored secret flow of arms from Libya to the Syrian opposition, via Turkey, had been underway for more than a year (it started sometime after Gaddafi's death on October 20, 2011). The operation was largely run out of a covert CIA annex in Benghazi, with State Department acquiescence. On September 11, 2012, the US ambassador to Libya,

Christopher Stevens, was killed during an anti-American demonstration that led to the burning down of the US consulate in Benghazi; reporters for the *Washington Post* found copies of the ambassador's schedule in the building's ruins. It showed that on September 10 Stevens had met with the chief of the CIA's annex operation. The next day, shortly before he died, he met a representative from Al-Marfa Shipping and Maritime Services, a Tripoli-based company which, the JCS adviser said, was known by the Joint Staff to be handling the weapons shipments.

By the late summer of 2013, the DIA's assessment had been circulated widely, but although many in the American intelligence community were aware that the Syrian opposition was dominated by extremists the CIA-sponsored weapons kept coming, presenting a continuing problem for Assad's army. Gaddafi's stockpile had created an international arms bazaar, though prices were high. "There was no way to stop the arms shipments that had been authorized by the president," the JCS adviser said. "The solution involved an appeal to the pocketbook. The CIA was approached by a representative from the Joint Chiefs with a suggestion: there were far less costly weapons available in Turkish arsenals that could reach the Syrian rebels within days, and without a boat ride." But it wasn't only the CIA that benefited. "We worked with Turks we trusted who were not loyal to Erdoğan," the adviser said, "and got them to ship the jihadists in Syria all the obsolete weapons in the arsenal, including M1 carbines that hadn't been seen since the

Korean War and lots of Soviet arms. It was a message Assad could understand: 'We have the power to diminish a presidential policy in its tracks.' "

The flow of US intelligence to the Syrian army, and the downgrading of the quality of the arms being supplied to the rebels, came at a critical juncture. The Syrian army had suffered heavy losses in the spring of 2013 in fighting against Jabhat al-Nusra and other extremist groups as it failed to hold the provincial capital of Raqqa. Sporadic Syrian army and air-force raids continued in the area for months, with little success, until it was decided to withdraw from Raqqa and other hard to defend, lightly populated areas in the north and west and focus instead on consolidating the government's hold on Damascus and the heavily populated areas linking the capital to Latakia in the northeast. But as the army gained in strength with the Joint Chiefs' support, Saudi Arabia, Qatar and Turkey escalated their financing and arming of Jabhat al-Nusra and Islamic State, which by the end of 2013 had made enormous gains on both sides of the Syria/Iraq border. The remaining nonfundamentalist rebels found themselves fighting—and losing—pitched battles against the extremists. In January 2014, IS took complete control of Raqqa and the tribal areas around it from al-Nusra and established the city as its base. Assad still controlled 80 percent of the Syrian population, but he had lost a vast amount of territory.

CIA efforts to train the moderate rebel forces were also failing badly. "The CIA's training camp was in

Jordan and was controlled by a Syrian tribal group," the JCS adviser said. There was a suspicion that some of those who signed up for training were actually Syrian army regulars minus their uniforms. This had happened before, at the height of the Iraqi war, when hundreds of Shia militia members showed up at American training camps for new uniforms, weapons and a few days of training, and then disappeared into the desert. A separate training program, set up by the Pentagon in Turkey, fared no better. The Pentagon acknowledged in September that only "four or five" of its recruits were still battling Islamic State; a few days later 70 of them defected to Jabhat al-Nusra immediately after crossing the border into Syria.

In January 2014, despairing at the lack of progress, John Brennan, the director of the CIA, summoned American and Sunni Arab intelligence chiefs from throughout the Middle East to a secret meeting in Washington, with the aim of persuading Saudi Arabia to stop supporting extremist fighters in Syria. "The Saudis told us they were happy to listen," the JCS adviser said, "so everyone sat around in Washington to hear Brennan tell them that they had to get on board with the so-called moderates. His message was that if everyone in the region stopped supporting al-Nusra and ISIS their ammunition and weapons would dry up, and the moderates would win out." Brennan's message was ignored by the Saudis, the adviser said, who "went back home and increased their efforts with the extremists and asked us for more technical support. And we say OK, and so it turns out that we end up reinforcing the extremists."

But the Saudis were far from the only problem: American intelligence had accumulated intercept and human intelligence demonstrating that the Erdoğan government had been supporting Jabhat al-Nusra for years, and was now doing the same for Islamic State. "We can handle the Saudis," the adviser said. "We can handle the Muslim Brotherhood. You can argue that the whole balance in the Middle East is based on a form of mutually assured destruction between Israel and the rest of the Middle East, and Turkey can disrupt the balance—which is Erdoğan's dream. We told him we wanted him to shut down the pipeline of foreign jihadists flowing into Turkey. But he is dreaming big—of restoring the Ottoman Empire—and he did not realize the extent to which he could be successful in this."

One of the constants in US affairs since the fall of the Soviet Union has been a military-to-military relationship with Russia. After 1991 the US spent billions of dollars to help Russia secure its nuclear weapons complex, including a highly secret joint operation to remove weapons-grade uranium from unsecured storage depots in Kazakhstan. Joint programs to monitor the security of weapons-grade materials continued for the next two decades. During the American war on Afghanistan, Russia provided overflight rights for US cargo carriers and tankers, as well as access for the flow of weapons, ammunition, food and water the US war machine needed daily. Russia's military provided intelligence on Osama bin Laden's whereabouts and helped the US negotiate rights to use an airbase in Kyrgyzstan. The Joint Chiefs have been in communication with their Russian counterparts throughout the Syrian war, and the ties between the two militaries start at the top. In August, a few weeks before his retirement as chairman of the Joint Chiefs, Dempsey made a farewell visit to the headquarters of the Irish Defence Forces in Dublin and told his audience there that he had made a point while in office to keep in touch with the chief of the Russian General Staff, General Valery Gerasimov. "I've actually suggested to him that we not end our careers as we began them," Dempsey said—one a tank commander in West Germany, the other in the east.

When it comes to tackling Islamic State, Russia and the US have much to offer each other. Many in the IS leadership and rank and file fought for more than a decade against Russia in the two Chechen wars that began in 1994, and the Putin government is heavily invested in combating Islamist terrorism. "Russia knows the ISIS leadership," the JCS adviser said, "and has insights into its operational techniques, and has much intelligence to share." In return, he said, "we've got excellent trainers with years of experience in training foreign fighters— experience that Russia does not have." The adviser would not discuss what American intelligence is also believed to have: an ability to obtain targeting data, often by paying huge sums of cash, from sources within rebel militias.

A former White House adviser on Russian affairs told me that before 9/11 Putin "used to say to us: 'We have the same nightmares about different places.' He was referring to his problems with the caliphate in Chechnya and our early issues with al-Qaida. These days, after the Metrojet bombing over Sinai and the massacres in Paris and elsewhere, it's hard to avoid the conclusion that we actually have the same nightmares about the same places."

Yet the Obama administration continues to condemn Russia for its support of Assad. A retired senior diplomat who served at the US embassy in Moscow expressed sympathy for Obama's dilemma as the leader of the Western coalition opposed to Russia's aggression against Ukraine: "Ukraine is a serious issue and Obama has been handling it firmly with sanctions. But our policy vis-à-vis Russia is too often unfocused. But it's not about us in Syria. It's about making sure Bashar does not lose. The reality is that Putin does not want to see the chaos in Syria spread to Jordan or Lebanon, as it has to Iraq, and he does not want to see Syria end up in the hands of Isis. The most counterproductive thing Obama has done, and it has hurt our efforts to end the fighting a lot, was to say: 'Assad must go as a premise for negotiation.'" He also echoed a view held by some in the Pentagon when he alluded to a collateral factor behind Russia's decision to launch air strikes in support of the Syrian army on September 30: Putin's desire to prevent Assad from suffering the same fate as Gaddafi. He had been told that

Putin had watched a video of Gaddafi's savage death three times, a video that shows him being sodomized with a bayonet. The JCS adviser also told me of a US intelligence assessment which concluded that Putin had been appalled by Gaddafi's fate: "Putin blamed himself for letting Gaddafi go, for not playing a strong role behind the scenes" at the UN when the Western coalition was lobbying to be allowed to undertake the air strikes that destroyed the regime. "Putin believed that unless he got engaged Bashar would suffer the same fate—mutilated —and he'd see the destruction of his allies in Syria."

In a speech on November 22, Obama declared that the "principal targets" of the Russian air strikes "have been the moderate opposition." It's a line that the administration—along with most of the mainstream American media—has rarely strayed from. The Russians insist that they are targeting all rebel groups that threaten Syria's stability—including Islamic State. The Kremlin adviser on the Middle East explained in an interview that the first round of Russian air strikes was aimed at bolstering security around a Russian airbase in Latakia, an Alawite stronghold. The strategic goal, he said, has been to establish a jihadist-free corridor from Damascus to Latakia and the Russian naval base at Tartus and then to shift the focus of bombing gradually to the south and east, with a greater concentration of bombing missions over IS-held territory. Russian strikes on IS targets in and near Raqqa were reported as early as the beginning of October; in November there were further strikes on IS positions near the historic city of Palmyra and in Idlib province, a bitterly contested stronghold on the Turkish border.

Russian incursions into Turkish airspace began soon after Putin authorized the bombings, and the Russian air force deployed electronic jamming systems that interfered with Turkish radar. The message being sent to the Turkish air force, the JCS adviser said, was "We're going to fly our fighter planes where we want and when we want and jam your radar. Do not fuck with us! Putin was letting the Turks know what they were up against." Russia's aggression led to Turkish complaints and Russian denials, along with more aggressive border patrolling by the Turkish air force. There were no significant incidents until November 24, when two Turkish F-16 fighters, apparently acting under more aggressive rules of engagement, shot down a Russian Su-24M jet that had crossed into Turkish airspace for no more than 17 seconds. In the days after the fighter was shot down, Obama expressed support for Erdoğan, and after they met in private on December 1 he told a press conference that his administration remained "very much committed to Turkey's security and its sovereignty." He said that as long as Russia remained allied with Assad, "a lot of Russian resources are still going to be targeted at opposition groups ... that we support ... So I don't think we should be under any illusions that somehow Russia starts hitting only ISIL targets. That's not happening now. It was never happening. It's not going to be happening in the next several weeks."

The Kremlin adviser on the Middle East, like the
Joint Chiefs and the DIA, dismisses the "moderates" who
have Obama's support, seeing them as extremist Islamist groups that fight alongside Jabhat al-Nusra and ISIS
("There's no need to play with words and split terrorists into moderate and not moderate," Putin said in a
speech on October 22.) The American generals see them
as exhausted militias that have been forced to make an
accommodation with Jabhat al-Nusra or ISIS in order
to survive. At the end of 2014, Jürgen Todenhöfer, a
German journalist who was allowed to spend ten days
touring ISIS-held territory in Iraq and Syria, told CNN
that the ISIS leadership "are all laughing about the Free
Syrian Army. They don't take them for serious. They say:
"The best arms sellers we have are the FSA. If they get a
good weapon, they sell it to us." They didn't take them
for serious. They take for serious Assad. They take for
serious, of course, the bombs. But they fear nothing, and
FSA doesn't play a role."

Putin's bombing campaign provoked a series of anti-
Russia articles in the American press. On October 25,
the *New York Times* reported, citing Obama administration officials, that Russian submarines and spy ships
were "aggressively" operating near the undersea cables
that carry much of the world's Internet traffic—although,
as the article went on to acknowledge, there was "no evidence yet" of any Russian attempt actually to interfere
with that traffic. Ten days earlier the *Times* published

a summary of Russian intrusions into its former Soviet satellite republics, and described the Russian bombing in Syria as being "in some respects a return to the ambitious military moves of the Soviet past." The report did not note that the Assad administration had invited Russia to intervene, nor did it mention the US bombing raids inside Syria that had been underway since the previous September, without Syria's approval. An October op-ed in the same paper by Michael McFaul, Obama's ambassador to Russia between 2012 and 2014, declared that the Russian air campaign was attacking "everyone except the Islamic State." The anti-Russia stories did not abate after the Metrojet disaster, for which Islamic State claimed credit. Few in the US government and media questioned why IS would target a Russian airliner, along with its 224 passengers and crew, if Moscow's air force was attacking only the Syrian "moderates."

Economic sanctions, meanwhile, are still in effect against Russia for what a large number of Americans consider Putin's war crimes in Ukraine, as are US Treasury Department sanctions against Syria and against those Americans who do business there. The *New York Times*, in a report on sanctions in late November, revived an old and groundless assertion, saying that the Treasury's actions "emphasize an argument that the administration has increasingly been making about Mr Assad as it seeks to press Russia to abandon its backing for him: that although he professes to be at war with Islamist terrorists, he has a symbiotic relationship with the Islamic

State that has allowed it to thrive while he has clung to power."

The four core elements of Obama's Syria policy remain intact today: an insistence that Assad must go; that no anti-IS coalition with Russia is possible; that Turkey is a steadfast ally in the war against terrorism; and that there really are significant moderate opposition forces for the US to support. The Paris attacks on November 13 that killed 130 people did not change the White House's public stance, although many European leaders, including François Hollande, advocated greater cooperation with Russia and agreed to coordinate more closely with its air force; there was also talk of the need to be more flexible about the timing of Assad's exit from power. On November 24, Hollande flew to Washington to discuss how France and the US could collaborate more closely in the fight against Islamic State. At a joint press conference at the White House, Obama said he and Hollande had agreed that "Russia's strikes against the moderate opposition only bolster the Assad regime, whose brutality has helped to fuel the rise" of IS. Hollande didn't go that far but he said that the diplomatic process in Vienna would "lead to Bashar al-Assad's departure … a government of unity is required." The press conference failed to deal with the far more urgent impasse between the two men on the matter of Erdoğan. Obama defended Turkey's right to defend its borders; Hollande said it was "a matter of urgency" for Turkey to take action against terrorists. The JCS adviser told me that one of Hollande's main goals in flying to Washington had been to try to persuade Obama to join the EU in a mutual declaration of war against Islamic State. Obama said no. The Europeans had pointedly not gone to NATO, to which Turkey belongs, for such a declaration. "Turkey is the problem," the JCS adviser said.

Assad, naturally, doesn't accept that a group of foreign leaders should be deciding on his future. Imad Moustapha, now Syria's ambassador to China, was dean of the IT faculty at the University of Damascus, and a close aide of Assad's, when he was appointed in 2004 as the Syrian ambassador to the US, a post he held for seven years. Moustapha is known still to be close to Assad and can be trusted to reflect what he thinks. He told me that for Assad to surrender power would mean capitulating to "armed terrorist groups" and that ministers in a national unity government—such as was being proposed by the Europeans—would be seen to be beholden to the foreign powers that appointed them. These powers could remind the new president "that they could easily replace him as they did before to the predecessor … Assad owes it to his people: he could not leave because the historic enemies of Syria are demanding his departure."

Moustapha also brought up China, an ally of Assad that has allegedly committed more than $30 billion to postwar reconstruction in Syria. China, too, is worried about Islamic State. "China regards the Syrian crisis from three perspectives," he said: international law and legitimacy; global strategic positioning; and the activities of jihadist Uighurs, from Xinjiang province in China's far west. Xinjiang borders eight nations—Mongolia, Russia, Kazakhstan, Kyrgyzstan, Tajikistan, Afghanistan, Pakistan and India—and, in China's view, serves as a funnel for terrorism around the world and within China. Many Uighur fighters now in Syria are known to be members of the East Turkestan Islamic Movement—an often violent separatist organization that seeks to establish an Islamist Uighur state in Xinjiang. "The fact that they have been aided by Turkish intelligence to move from China into Syria through Turkey has caused a tremendous amount of tension between the Chinese and Turkish intelligence," Moustapha said. "China is concerned that the Turkish role of supporting the Uighur fighters in Syria may be extended in the future to support Turkey's agenda in Xinjiang. We are already providing the Chinese intelligence service with information regarding these terrorists and the routes they crossed from on traveling into Syria."

Moustapha's concerns were echoed by a Washington foreign affairs analyst who has closely followed the passage of jihadists through Turkey and into Syria. The analyst, whose views are routinely sought by senior government officials, told me that "Erdoğan has been bringing Uighurs into Syria by special transport while his government has been agitating in favor of their struggle in China. Uighur and Burmese Muslim terrorists who escape into Thailand somehow get Turkish passports and are then flown to Turkey for transit into Syria." He added that there was also what amounted to another "rat line" that was funneling Uighurs—estimates range from a few hundred to many thousands over the years—from China into Kazakhstan for eventual relay to Turkey, and then to IS territory in Syria. "US intelligence," he said, "is not getting good information about these activities because those insiders who are unhappy with the policy are not talking to them." He also said it was "not clear" that the officials responsible for Syrian policy in the State Department and White House "get it." *IHS-Jane's Defence Weekly* estimated in October 2015 that as many as five thousand Uighur would-be fighters have arrived in Turkey since 2013, with perhaps two thousand moving on to Syria. Moustapha said he has information that "up to 860 Uighur fighters are currently in Syria."

China's growing concern about the Uighur problem and its link to Syria and Islamic State have preoccupied Christina Lin, a scholar who dealt with Chinese issues a decade ago while serving in the Pentagon under Donald Rumsfeld. "I grew up in Taiwan and came to the Pentagon as a critic of China," Lin told me. "I used to demonize the Chinese as ideologues, and they are not perfect. But over the years as I see them opening up and evolving, I have begun to change my perspective. I see China as a potential partner for various global challenges, especially in the Middle East. There are many places—Syria for one—where the United States and China must cooperate in regional security and counterterrorism." A few weeks earlier, she said, China and India, Cold War enemies that "hated each other more than China and the United States hated each other, conducted a series of joint counter-terrorism exercises. And today China and Russia both want to cooperate on terrorism issues with the United States." As China sees it, Lin suggests, Uighur militants who have made their way to Syria are being trained by Islamic State in survival techniques intended to aid them on covert return trips to the Chinese mainland, for future terrorist attacks there. "If Assad fails," Lin wrote in a paper published in September, "jihadi fighters from Russia's Chechnya, China's Xinjiang and India's Kashmir will then turn their eyes towards the home front to con-tinue jihad, supported by a new and well-sourced Syrian operating base in the heart of the Middle East."

General Dempsey and his colleagues on the Joint Chiefs of Staff kept their dissent out of bureaucratic channels, and survived in office. General Michael Flynn did not. "Flynn incurred the wrath of the White House by insist-ing on telling the truth about Syria," said Patrick Lang, a retired army colonel who served for nearly a decade as the chief Middle East civilian intelligence officer for the DIA. "He thought truth was the best thing and they shoved him out. He wouldn't shut up." Flynn told me his problems went beyond Syria. "I was shaking things up at the DIA—and not just moving deck chairs on the *Titanic*. It was radical reform. I felt that the civilian leadership did not want to hear the truth. I suffered for it, but I'm OK with that." In a recent interview in *Der Spiegel*, Flynn was blunt about Russia's entry into the Syrian war: "We have to work constructively with Russia. Whether we like it or not, Russia made a decision to be there and to act militarily. They are there, and this has dramatically changed the dynamic. So you can't say Russia is bad; they have to go home. It's not going to happen. Get real."

Few in the US Congress share this view. One exception is Tulsi Gabbard, a Democrat from Hawaii and member of the House Armed Services Committee who, as a major in the Army National Guard, served two tours in the Middle East. In an interview on CNN in October she said: "The US and the CIA should stop this illegal and counterproductive war to overthrow the Syrian government of Assad and should stay focused on fighting against ... the Islamic extremist groups."

"Does it not concern you," the interviewer asked, "that Assad's regime has been brutal, killing at least 200,000 and maybe 300,000 of his own people?"

"The things that are being said about Assad right now," Gabbard responded, "are the same that were said about Gaddafi, they are the same things that were said about Saddam Hussein by those who were advocating for the US to ... overthrow those regimes ... If it happens here in Syria ... we will end up in a situation with far greater suffering, with far greater persecution of religious minorities and Christians in Syria, and our enemy will be far stronger."

"So what you are saying," the interviewer asked, "is that the Russian military involvement in the air and on-the-ground Iranian involvement—they are actually doing the US a favor?"

"They are working toward defeating our common enemy," Gabbard replied.

Gabbard later told me that many of her colleagues in Congress, Democrats and Republicans, have thanked her privately for speaking out. "There are a lot of people in the general public, and even in the Congress, who need to have things clearly explained to them," Gabbard said. "But it's hard when there's so much deception about what is going on. The truth is not out." It's unusual for a politician to challenge her party's foreign policy directly and on the record. For someone on the inside, with access to the most secret intelligence, speaking openly and critically can be a career-ender. Informed dissent can be transmitted by means of a trust relationship between a reporter and those on the inside, but it almost invariably includes no signature. The dissent exists, however. The longtime consultant to the Joint Special Operations Command could not hide his contempt when I asked him for his view of the US's Syria policy. "The solution in Syria is right before our nose," he said. "Our primary threat is ISIS and all of us—the United States, Russia and China—need to work together. Bashar will remain in office and, after the country is stabilized there will be an election. There is no other option."

The military's indirect pathway to Assad disappeared

with Dempsey's retirement in September. His replacement as chairman of the Joint Chiefs, General Joseph Dunford, testified before the Senate Armed Services Committee in July, two months before assuming office. "If you want to talk about a nation that could pose an existential threat to the United States, I'd have to point to Russia," Dunford said. "If you look at their behavior, it's nothing short of alarming." In October, as chairman, Dunford dismissed the Russian bombing efforts in Syria, telling the same committee that Russia "is not fighting" IS. He added that America must "work with Turkish partners to secure the northern border of Syria" and "do all we can to enable vetted Syrian opposition forces"— i.e., the "moderates"—to fight the extremists.

Obama now has a more compliant Pentagon. There will be no more indirect challenges from the military leadership to his policy of disdain for Assad and support for Erdoğan. Dempsey and his associates remain mystified by Obama's continued public defense of Erdoğan, given the American intelligence community's strong case against him—and the evidence that Obama, in private, accepts that case. "We know what you're doing with the radicals in Syria," the president told Erdoğan's intelligence chief at a tense meeting at the White House (as I reported in Chapter 2). The Joint Chiefs and the DIA were constantly telling Washington's leadership of the jihadist threat in Syria, and of Turkey's support for it. The message was never listened to. Why not?

Index